Vegetables & Salads

Publisher & Creative Director: Nick Wells
Senior Editor: Sarah Goulding
Designer: Mike Spender
With thanks to: Gina Steer

This is a **FLAME TREE** Book

FLAME TREE PUBLISHING
Crabtree Hall, Crabtree Lane
Fulham, London SW6 6TY
United Kingdom
www.flametreepublishing.com

Flame Tree is part of The Foundry Creative Media Company Limited

First published 2006

07 09 10 08 06
1 3 5 7 9 10 8 6 4 2

ISBN-10 1 84451 524 9
ISBN-13 978 184451 524 0

A copy of the CIP data for this book is available from the British Library.

Printed in China

Vegetables & Salads

Quick and Easy, Proven Recipes

FLAME TREE
PUBLISHING

Contents

Contents

Contents

Hygiene in the Kitchen

It is well worth remembering that many foods can carry some form of bacteria. In most cases, the worst it will lead to is a bout of food poisoning or gastroenteritis, although for certain groups this can be more serious. The risk can be reduced or eliminated by good food hygiene and proper cooking.

Do not buy food that is past its sell-by date and do not consume any food that is past its use-by date. When buying food, use the eyes and nose. If the food looks tired, limp or a bad colour or it has a rank, acrid or simply bad smell, do not buy or eat it under any circumstances.

Regularly clean, defrost and clear out the refrigerator or freezer – it is worth checking the packaging to see exactly how long each product is safe to freeze.

Dish cloths and tea towels must be washed and changed regularly. Ideally use disposable cloths which should be replaced on a daily basis. More durable cloths should be left

to soak in bleach, then washed in the washing machine on a boil wash.

Always keep your hands, cooking utensils and food preparation surfaces clean and never allow pets to climb on to any work surfaces.

Buying

Avoid bulk buying where possible, especially fresh produce such as meat, poultry, fish, fruit and vegetables unless buying for the freezer. Fresh foods lose their nutritional value rapidly so buying a little at a time minimises loss of nutrients. It also eliminates a packed refrigerator which reduces the effectiveness of the refrigeration process.

When buying frozen foods, ensure that they are not heavily iced on the outside. Place in the freezer as soon as possible after purchase.

Preparation

Make sure that all work surfaces and utensils are clean and dry. Separate chopping boards should be used for raw and cooked meats, fish and vegetables. It is worth washing all fruits and vegetables regardless of whether they are going to be eaten raw or lightly cooked. Do not reheat food more than once.

All poultry must be thoroughly thawed before cooking. Leave the food in the refrigerator until it is completely thawed. Once defrosted, the chicken should be cooked as soon as possible. The only time food can be refrozen is when the food has been thoroughly thawed then cooked. Once the food has cooled then it can be frozen again for one month.

All poultry and game (except for duck) must be cooked

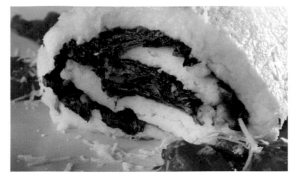

thoroughly. When cooked the juices will run clear. Other meats, like minced meat and pork should be cooked right the way through. Fish should turn opaque, be firm in texture and break easily into large flakes.

Storing, Refrigerating and Freezing

Meat, poultry, fish, seafood and dairy products should all be refrigerated. The temperature of the refrigerator should be between 1–5°C/34–41°F while the freezer temperature should not rise above -18°C/-0.4°F. When refrigerating cooked food, allow it to cool down quickly and completely before refrigerating. Hot food will raise the temperature of the refrigerator and possibly affect or spoil other food stored in it.

Food within the refrigerator and freezer should always be covered. Raw and cooked food should be stored in separate parts of the refrigerator. Cooked food should be kept on the top shelves of the refrigerator, while raw meat, poultry and fish should be placed on bottom shelves to avoid drips and cross-contamination.

High-Risk Foods

Certain foods may carry risks to people who are considered vulnerable such as the elderly, the ill, pregnant women, babies and those suffering from a recurring illness. It is advisable to avoid those foods which belong to a higher-risk category.

There is a slight chance that some eggs carry the bacteria salmonella. Cook the eggs until both the yolk and the white are firm to eliminate this risk. Sauces including Hollandaise, mayonnaise, mousses, soufflés and meringues all use raw or lightly cooked eggs, as do custard-based dishes, ice creams and sorbets. These are all considered high-risk foods to the vulnerable groups mentioned above. Certain meats and poultry also carry the potential risk of salmonella and so should be cooked thoroughly until the juices run clear and there is no pinkness left. Unpasteurised products such as milk, cheese (especially soft cheese), pâté, meat (both raw and cooked) all have the potential risk of listeria and should be avoided.

When buying seafood, buy from a reputable source. Fish should have bright clear eyes, shiny skin and bright pink or red gills. The fish should feel stiff to the touch, with a slight smell of sea air and iodine. The flesh of fish steaks and fillets should be translucent with no signs of discolouration. Avoid any molluscs that are open or do not close when tapped lightly. Univalves such as cockles or winkles should withdraw into their shells when lightly prodded. Squid and octopus should have firm flesh and a pleasant sea smell.

Care is required when freezing seafood. It is imperative to check whether the fish has been frozen before. If it has been, then it should not be frozen again under any circumstances.

Nutrition
The Role of Essential Nutrients

A healthy and well-balanced diet is the body's primary energy source. In children, it constitutes the building blocks for future health as well as providing lots of energy. In adults, it encourages self-healing and regeneration within the body. A well-balanced diet will provide the body with all the essential nutrients it needs. This can be achieved by eating a variety of foods, demonstrated in the pyramid below:

Fats

milk, yogurt
and cheese

Proteins

meat, fish, poultry, eggs,
nuts and pulses

*Fruits and
Vegetables*

Starchy Carbohydrates

cereals, potatoes, bread, rice and pasta

Fats

Fats fall into two categories: saturated and unsaturated fats. It is very important that a healthy balance is achieved within the diet. Fats are an essential part of the diet and a source of energy and provide essential fatty acids and fat soluble vitamins. The right balance of fats should boost the body's immunity to infection and keep muscles, nerves and arteries in good condition. Saturated fats are of animal origin and are hard when stored at room temperature. They can be found in dairy produce, meat, eggs, margarines and hard white cooking fat (lard) as well as in manufactured products such as pies, biscuits and cakes. A high intake of saturated fat over many years has been proven to increase heart disease and high blood cholesterol levels and often leads to weight gain. The aim of a healthy diet is to keep the fat content low in the foods that we eat. Lowering the amount of saturated fat that we consume is very important, but this does not mean that it is good to consume lots of other types of fat.

There are two kinds of unsaturated fats: poly-unsaturated fats and monounsaturated fats. Poly-unsaturated fats include the following oils: safflower oil, soybean oil, corn oil and sesame oil. Within the poly-unsaturated group are Omega oils. The Omega-3 oils are of significant interest because they have been found to be particularly beneficial to coronary health and can encourage brain growth and development. Omega-3 oils are derived from oily fish such as salmon, mackerel, herring, pilchards and sardines. It is recommended that we should eat these types of fish at least once a week. However, for those who do not eat fish or who are vegetarians, liver oil supplements are available in most supermarkets and health shops. It is suggested that these supplements should be taken on a daily basis. The most popular oils that are high in monounsaturates are olive oil, sunflower oil and peanut oil. The Mediterranean diet, which is based on a diet high in mono-unsaturated fats, is recommended for heart health. Also, monounsaturated fats are known to help reduce the levels of LDL (the bad) cholestrol.

Proteins

Composed of amino acids (proteins' building bricks), proteins perform a wide variety of essential functions for the body including supplying energy and building and repairing tissues. Good sources of proteins are eggs, milk, yogurt, cheese, meat, fish, poultry, eggs, nuts and pulses. (See the second level of the pyramid.) Some of these foods, however, contain saturated fats. To strike a nutritional balance eat generous amounts of vegetable protein foods such as soya, beans, lentils, peas and nuts.

Fruits and Vegetables

Not only are fruits and vegetables the most visually appealing foods, but they are extremely good for us, providing essential vitamins and minerals essential for growth, repair and protection in the human body. Fruits and vegetables are low in calories and

are responsible for regulating the body's metabolic processes and controlling the composition of its fluids and cells.

Minerals

CALCIUM Important for healthy bones and teeth, nerve transmission, muscle contraction, blood clotting and hormone function. Calcium promotes a healthy heart, improves skin, relieves aching muscles and bones, maintains the correct acid-alkaline balance and reduces menstrual cramps. Good sources are dairy products, small bones of small fish, nuts, pulses, fortified white flours, breads and green leafy vegetables.

CHROMIUM Part of the glucose tolerance factor, chromium balances blood sugar levels, helps to normalise hunger and reduce cravings, improves lifespan, helps protect DNA and is essential for heart function. Good sources are brewer's yeast, wholemeal bread, rye bread, oysters, potatoes, green peppers, butter and parsnips.

IODINE Important for the manufacture of thyroid hormones and for normal development. Good sources of iodine are seafood, seaweed, milk and dairy products.

IRON As a component of haemoglobin, iron carries oxygen around the body. It is vital for normal growth and development. Good sources are liver, corned beef, red meat, fortified breakfast cereals, pulses, green leafy vegetables, egg yolk and cocoa and cocoa products.

MAGNESIUM Important for efficient functioning of metabolic enzymes and development of the skeleton. Magnesium promotes healthy muscles by helping them to relax and is therefore good for PMS. It is also important for heart muscles and the nervous system. Good sources are nuts, green vegetables, meat, cereals, milk and yogurt.

PHOSPHORUS Forms and maintains bones and teeth, builds muscle tissue, helps maintain the body's pH and aids metabolism and energy production. Phosphorus is present in almost all foods.

POTASSIUM Enables nutrients to move into cells, while waste products move out; promotes healthy nerves and muscles; maintains fluid balance in the body; helps secretion of insulin for blood sugar control to produce constant energy; relaxes muscles; maintains heart functioning and stimulates gut movement to encourage proper elimination. Good sources are fruit, vegetables, milk and bread.

SELENIUM Antioxidant properties help to protect against free radicals and carcinogens. Selenium reduces inflammation, stimulates the immune system to fight infections, promotes a healthy heart and helps vitamin E's action. It is also required for the male reproductive system and is needed for metabolism. Good sources are tuna, liver, kidney, meat, eggs, cereals, nuts and dairy products.

SODIUM Important in helping to control body fluid and balance, preventing dehydration. Sodium is involved in muscle and nerve function and helps move nutrients into cells. All foods are good sources, however processed, pickled and salted foods are richest in sodium.

ZINC Important for metabolism and the healing of wounds. It also aids ability to cope with stress, promotes a healthy

nervous system and brain especially in the growing foetus, aids bones and teeth formation and is essential for constant energy. Good sources are liver, meat, pulses, whole-grain cereals, nuts and oysters.

Vitamins

VITAMIN A Important for cell growth and development and for the formation of visual pigments in the eye. Vitamin A comes in two forms: retinol and beta-carotenes. Retinol is found in liver, meat and meat products and whole milk and its products. Beta-carotene is a powerul antioxidant and is found in red and yellow fruits and vegetables such as carrots, mangoes and apricots.

VITAMIN B1 Important in releasing energy from carboydrate-containing foods. Good sources are yeast and yeast products, bread, fortified breakfast cereals and potatoes.

VITAMIN B2 Important for metabolism of proteins, fats and carbohydrates to produce energy. Good sources are meat, yeast extracts, fortified breakfast cereals and milk and its products.

VITAMIN B3 Required for the metabolism of food into energy production. Good sources are milk and milk products, fortified breakfast cereals, pulses, meat, poultry and eggs.

VITAMIN B5 Important for the metabolism of food and energy production. All foods are good sources but especially fortified breakfast cereals, whole-grain bread and dairy products.

VITAMIN B6 Important for metabolism of protein and fat. Vitamin B6 may also be involved with the regulation of sex hormones. Good sources are liver, fish, pork, soya beans and peanuts.

VITAMIN B12 Important for the production of red blood cells and DNA. It is vital for growth and the nervous system. Good sources are meat, fish, eggs, poultry and milk.

BIOTIN Important for metabolism of fatty acids. Good sources of biotin are liver, kidney, eggs and nuts. Micro-organisms also manufacture this vitamin in the gut.

VITAMIN C Important for healing wounds and the formation of collagen which keeps skin and bones strong. It is an important antioxidant. Good sources are fruits, soft summer fruits and vegetables.

VITAMIN D Important for absorption and handling of calcium to help build bone strength. Good sources are oily fish, eggs, whole milk and milk products, margarine and of course sufficient exposure to sunlight, as vitamin D is made in the skin.

VITAMIN E Important as an antioxidant vitamin helping to protect cell membranes from damage. Good sources are vegetable oils, margarines, seeds, nuts and green vegetables.

FOLIC ACID Critical during pregnancy for the development of the brain and nerves. It is always essential for brain and nerve function and is needed for utilising protein and red blood cell formation. Good sources are whole-grain cereals, fortified breakfast cereals, green leafy vegetables, oranges and liver.

VITAMIN K Important for controlling blood clotting. Good sources are cauliflower, Brussels sprouts, lettuce, cabbage, beans, broccoli, peas, asparagus, potatoes, corn oil, tomatoes and milk.

Carbohydrates

Carbohydrates are an energy source and come in two forms: starch and sugar carbohydrates. Starch carbohydrates are also known as complex carbohydrates and they include all cereals, potatoes, breads, rice and pasta. (See the fourth level of the pyramid). Eating whole-grain varieties of these foods also provides fibre. Diets high in fibre are believed to be beneficial in helping to prevent bowel cancer and can also keep cholesterol down. High-fibre diets are also good for those concerned about weight gain. Fibre is bulky so fills the stomach, therefore reducing hunger pangs. Sugar carbohydrates, which are also known as fast-release carbohydrates (because of the quick fix of energy they give to the body), include sugar and sugar-sweetened products such as jams and syrups. Milk provides lactose, which is a milk sugar, and fruits provide fructose, which is a fruit sugar.

Fish & Shellfish

Seafood Noodle Salad

SERVES 4

8 baby squid, cleaned
2 tbsp mirin
2 tbsp rice vinegar
4 tbsp sunflower oil
1 red chilli, deseeded and
    finely chopped
2 garlic cloves, peeled
    and crushed

6 spring onions, trimmed
    and finely sliced
1 red pepper, deseeded and
    finely sliced
1 tbsp turmeric
2 tsp ground coriander
8 raw tiger prawns, peeled
175 g/6 oz medium

egg noodles
175 g/6 oz fresh
    white crabmeat
50 g/2 oz beansprouts
salt and freshly ground
    black pepper

Remove the tentacles from the squid and reserve. Slit the squid bodies open down one side and open out flat. Using a small sharp knife, score the flesh diagonally, first in one direction then the other, to make diamond shapes. Place in a bowl with the squid tentacles, mirin, rice vinegar, half the oil and the chilli and leave to marinate in the refrigerator for 1 hour.

Heat a wok until very hot. Add the remaining oil and, when hot, add the garlic, half the spring onions and the red pepper. Stir-fry for 1 minute, then add the turmeric and coriander. Cook for a further 30 seconds before adding the cleaned squid and its marinade and the prawns. Bring to the boil and simmer for 2–3 minutes, or until the squid and prawns are tender. Remove from the heat and leave to cool.

Cook the noodles for 3–4 minutes until tender, or according to packet directions. Drain well and put in a large serving bowl along with the white crabmeat and the cooled squid and prawn mixture. Stir together and leave until cold. Just before serving, add the beansprouts and remaining spring onions with seasoning to taste and serve.

 Try this: FOR AN ALTERNATIVE: 32   FOR ENTERTAINING: 52

Fried Whitebait with Rocket Salad

SERVES 4

450 g/1 lb whitebait, fresh
 or frozen
oil, for frying
85 g/3 oz plain flour
½ tsp of cayenne pepper
salt and freshly ground

black pepper

For the salad:
125 g/4 oz rocket leaves
125 g/4 oz cherry tomatoes,
 halved

75 g/3 oz cucumber,
 cut into dice
3 tbsp olive oil
1 tbsp fresh lemon juice
½ tsp Dijon mustard
½ tsp caster sugar

If the whitebait are frozen, thaw completely, then wipe dry with absorbent kitchen paper.

Start to heat the oil in a deep-fat fryer. Arrange the fish in a large, shallow dish and toss well in the flour, cayenne pepper and salt and pepper.

Deep fry the fish in batches for 2–3 minutes, or until crisp and golden. Keep the cooked fish warm while deep frying the remaining fish.

Meanwhile, to make the salad, arrange the rocket leaves, cherry tomatoes and cucumber on individual serving dishes. Whisk the olive oil and the remaining ingredients together and season lightly. Drizzle the dressing over the salad and serve with the whitebait.

Try this: FOR AN ALTERNATIVE: 120 FOR ENTERTAINING: 252

Marinated Mackerel with Tomato & Basil Salad

SERVES 3

3 mackerel, filleted
3 beefsteak tomatoes, sliced
50 g/2 oz watercress
2 oranges, peeled and
   segmented
75 g/3 oz mozzarella
   cheese, sliced
2 tbsp basil leaves, shredded

sprig of fresh basil,
   to garnish

For the marinade:
juice of 2 lemons
4 tbsp olive oil
4 tbsp basil leaves

For the dressing:
1 tbsp lemon juice
1 tsp Dijon mustard
1 tsp caster sugar
salt and freshly ground
   black pepper
5 tbsp olive oil

Remove as many of the fine pin bones as possible from the mackerel fillets, lightly rinse and pat dry with absorbent kitchen paper and place in a shallow dish.

Blend the marinade ingredients together and pour over the mackerel fillets. Make sure the marinade has covered the fish completely. Cover and leave in a cool place for at least 8 hours, but preferably overnight. As the fillets marinate, they will loose their translucency and look as if they are cooked.

Place the tomatoes, watercress, oranges and mozzarella cheese in a large bowl and toss. To make the dressing, whisk the lemon juice with the mustard, sugar and seasoning in a bowl. Pour over half the dressing, toss again and then arrange on a serving platter.

Remove the mackerel from the marinade, cut into bite-sized pieces and sprinkle with the shredded basil. Arrange on top of the salad, drizzle over the remaining dressing, scatter with basil leaves and garnish with a basil sprig. Serve.

Try this: FOR AN ALTERNATIVE: 56   FOR ENTERTAINING: 42

Warm Swordfish Niçoise

SERVES 4

4 swordfish steaks, about 2.5 cm/1 inch thick, weighing about 175 g/6 oz each	400 g/14 oz farfalle	225 g/8 oz ripe tomatoes, quartered
juice of 1 lime	225 g/8 oz French beans, topped and cut in half	50 g/2 oz pitted black olives
2 tbsp olive oil	1 tsp Dijon mustard	2 medium eggs, hard boiled and quartered
salt and freshly ground black pepper	2 tsp white wine vinegar	8 anchovy fillets, drained and cut in half lengthways
	pinch caster sugar	
	3 tbsp olive oil	

Place the swordfish steaks in a shallow dish. Mix the lime juice with the oil, season to taste with salt and pepper and spoon over the steaks. Turn the steaks to coat them evenly. Cover and place in the refrigerator to marinate for 1 hour.

Bring a large pan of lightly salted water to a rolling boil. Add the farfalle and cook according to the packet instructions, or until 'al dente'. Add the French beans about 4 minutes before the end of cooking time.

Mix the mustard, vinegar and sugar together in a small jug. Gradually whisk in the olive oil to make a thick dressing.

Cook the swordfish in a griddle pan or under a hot preheated grill for 2 minutes on each side, or until just cooked through; overcooking will make it tough and dry. Remove and cut into 2 cm/¾ inch chunks.

Drain the pasta and beans thoroughly and place in a large bowl. Pour over the dressing and toss to coat. Add the cooked swordfish, tomatoes, olives, hard-boiled eggs and anchovy fillets. Gently toss together, taking care not to break up the eggs. Tip into a warmed serving bowl or divide the pasta between individual plates. Serve immediately.

Try this: FOR AN ALTERNATIVE: 110 FOR ENTERTAINING: 136

Mixed Salad with Anchovy Dressing & Ciabatta Croûtons

SERVES 4

1 small head endive
1 small head chicory
1 fennel bulb
400 g can artichokes,
    drained and rinsed
½ cucumber
125 g/4 oz cherry tomatoes

75 g/3 oz black olives

For the anchovy dressing:
50 g can anchovy fillets
1 tsp Dijon mustard
1 small garlic clove, peeled
    and crushed

4 tbsp olive oil
1 tbsp lemon juice
freshly ground black pepper

For the ciabatta croûtons:
2 thick slices ciabatta bread
2 tbsp olive oil

Divide the endive and chicory into leaves and reserve some of the larger ones. Arrange the smaller leaves in a wide salad bowl.

Cut the fennel bulb in half from the stalk to the root end, then cut across in fine slices. Quarter the artichokes, then quarter and slice the cucumber and halve the tomatoes. Add to the salad bowl with the olives.

To make the dressing, drain the anchovies and put in a blender with the mustard, garlic, olive oil, lemon juice, 2 tablespoons of hot water and black pepper. Whiz together until smooth and thickened.

To make the croûtons, cut the bread into 1 cm/½ inch cubes. Heat the oil in a frying pan, add the bread cubes and fry for 3 minutes, turning frequently until golden. Remove and drain on absorbent kitchen paper.

Drizzle half the anchovy dressing over the prepared salad and toss to coat. Arrange the reserved endive and chicory leaves around the edge, then drizzle over the remaining dressing. Scatter over the croûtons and serve immediately.

Try this: FOR AN ALTERNATIVE: 22   FOR ENTERTAINING: 32

Ratatouille Mackerel

SERVES 4

1 red pepper
1 tbsp olive oil
1 red onion, peeled
1 garlic clove, peeled and
   thinly sliced
2 courgettes, trimmed and

cut into thick slices
400 g can chopped tomatoes
sea salt and freshly ground
   black pepper
4 x 275 g/10 oz small
   mackerel, cleaned and

heads removed
spray of olive oil
lemon juice for drizzling
12 fresh basil leaves
couscous or rice mixed with
   chopped parsley, to serve

Preheat the oven to 190°C/375°F/Gas Mark 5. Cut the top off the red pepper, remove the seeds and membrane, then cut into chunks. Cut the red onion into thick wedges.

Heat the oil in a large pan and cook the onion and garlic for 5 minutes or until beginning to soften. Add the pepper chunks and courgettes slices and cook for a further 5 minutes.

Pour in the chopped tomatoes with their juice and cook for a further 5 minutes. Season to taste with salt and pepper and pour into an ovenproof dish.

Season the fish with salt and pepper and arrange on top of the vegetables. Spray with a little olive oil and lemon juice. Cover and cook in the preheated oven for 20 minutes.

Remove the cover, add the basil leaves and return to the oven for a further 5 minutes. Serve immediately with couscous or rice mixed with parsley.

Try this: FOR AN ALTERNATIVE: 34 FOR ENTERTAINING: 30

Fish Lasagne

SERVES 4

75 g/3 oz mushrooms
1 tsp sunflower oil
1 small onion, peeled and
   finely chopped
1 tbsp freshly
   chopped oregano
400 g can chopped tomatoes
1 tbsp tomato purée

salt and freshly ground
   black pepper
450 g/1 lb cod or haddock
   fillets, skinned
9–12 sheets pre-cooked
   lasagne verde
For the topping:
1 medium egg, beaten

125 g/4 oz cottage cheese
150 ml/¼ pint natural yogurt
50 g/2 oz Cheddar
   cheese, grated

To serve:
mixed salad leaves
cherry tomatoes

Preheat the oven to 190˚C/375˚F/Gas Mark 5. Wipe the mushrooms, trim the stalks and chop. Heat the oil in a large heavy-based pan, add the onion and gently cook the onion for 3–5 minutes or until soft.

Stir in the mushrooms, the oregano and the chopped tomatoes with their juice. Blend the tomato purée with 1 tablespoon of water. Stir into the pan and season to taste with salt and pepper. Bring the sauce to the boil, then simmer uncovered for 5–10 minutes. Remove as many of the tiny pin bones as possible from the fish and cut into cubes and add to the tomato sauce mixture. Stir gently and remove the pan from the heat.

Cover the base of an ovenproof dish with two to three sheets of the lasagne verde. Top with half of the fish mixture. Repeat the layers finishing with the lasagne sheets.

To make the topping, mix together the beaten egg, cottage cheese and yogurt. Pour over the lasagne and sprinkle with the cheese. Cook the lasagne in the preheated oven for 40–45 minutes or until the topping is golden brown and bubbling. Serve the lasagne immediately with the mixed salad leaves and cherry tomatoes.

Try this: FOR AN ALTERNATIVE: 262 FOR ENTERTAINING: 322

Seared Scallop Salad

SERVES 4

12 king (large) scallops	2 tbsp balsamic vinegar	125 g/4 oz watercress
1 tbsp margerine or butter	1 tbsp clear honey	50 g/2 oz walnuts
2 tbsp orange juice	2 ripe pears, washed	freshly ground black pepper
	125 g/4 oz rocket	

Clean the scallops, removing the thin black vein from around the white meat and coral. Rinse thoroughly and dry on absorbent kitchen paper. Cut into 2–3 thick slices, depending on the scallop size.

Heat a griddle pan or heavy-based frying pan, then when hot, add the margerine or butter and allow to melt. Once melted, sear the scallops for 1 minute on each side or until golden. Remove from the pan and reserve.

Briskly whisk together the orange juice, balsamic vinegar and honey to make the dressing and reserve.

With a small, sharp knife carefully cut the pears into quarters, core then cut into chunks. Mix the rocket leaves, watercress, pear chunks and walnuts.

Pile on to serving plates and top with the scallops. Drizzle over the dressing and grind over plenty of black pepper. Serve immediately.

Try this: FOR AN ALTERNATIVE: 20 FOR ENTERTAINING: 304

Tuna & Mushroom Ragout

SERVES 4

225 g/8 oz basmati and
  wild rice
50 g/2 oz butter
1 tbsp olive oil
1 large onion, peeled and
  finely chopped
1 garlic clove, peeled
  and crushed
300 g/11 oz baby button

mushrooms, wiped
  and halved
2 tbsp plain flour
400 g can chopped tomatoes
1 tbsp freshly chopped
  parsley
dash of Worcestershire
  sauce
400 g can tuna in oil, drained

salt and freshly ground
  black pepper
4 tbsp Parmesan
  cheese, grated
1 tbsp freshly shredded basil

To serve:
green salad
garlic bread

Cook the basmati and wild rice in a saucepan of boiling salted water for 20 minutes, then drain and return to the pan. Stir in half of the butter, cover the pan and leave to stand for 2 minutes until all of the butter has melted.

Heat the oil and the remaining butter in a frying pan and cook the onion for 1–2 minutes until soft. Add the garlic and mushrooms and continue to cook for a further 3 minutes.

Stir in the flour and cook for 1 minute, then add the tomatoes and bring the sauce to the boil. Add the parsley, Worcestershire sauce and tuna and simmer gently for 3 minutes. Season to taste with salt and freshly ground pepper.

Stir the rice well, then spoon onto four serving plates and top with the tuna and mushroom mixture. Sprinkle with a spoonful of grated Parmesan cheese and some shredded basil for each portion and serve immediately with a green salad and chunks of garlic bread.

Try this: FOR AN ALTERNATIVE: 28   FOR ENTERTAINING: 318

Chunky Halibut Casserole

SERVES 6

50 g/2 oz butter
  or margarine
2 large onions, peeled and
  sliced into rings
1 red pepper, deseeded and
  roughly chopped
450 g/1 lb potatoes, peeled
450 g/1 lb courgettes,

trimmed and thickly sliced
2 tbsp plain flour
1 tbsp paprika
2 tsp vegetable oil
300 ml/½ pint white wine
150 ml/¼ pint fish stock
400 g can chopped tomatoes
2 tbsp freshly chopped basil

salt and freshly ground
  black pepper
450 g/1 lb halibut fillet,
  skinned and cut into
  2.5 cm/ 1 inch cubes
sprigs of fresh basil,
  to garnish
freshly cooked rice, to serve

Melt the butter or margarine in a large saucepan, add the onions and pepper and cook for 5 minutes, or until softened.

Cut the peeled potatoes into 2.5 cm/1 inch dice, rinse lightly and shake dry, then add them to the onions and pepper in the saucepan. Add the courgettes and cook, stirring frequently, for a further 2–3 minutes.

Sprinkle the flour, paprika and vegetable oil into the saucepan and cook, stirring continuously, for 1 minute. Pour in 150 ml/¼ pint of the wine, with all the stock and the chopped tomatoes, and bring to the boil.

Add the basil to the casserole, season to taste with salt and pepper and cover. Simmer for 15 minutes, then add the halibut and the remaining wine and simmer very gently for a further 5–7 minutes, or until the fish and vegetables are just tender. Garnish with basil sprigs and serve immediately with freshly cooked rice.

Try this: FOR AN ALTERNATIVE: 34   FOR ENTERTAINING: 44

Spanish Omelette with Smoked Cod

SERVES 3–4

3 tbsp sunflower oil
350 g/12 oz potatoes, peeled and cut into 1 cm/½ inch cubes
2 medium onions, peeled and cut into wedges
2–4 large garlic cloves, peeled and thinly sliced
1 large red pepper, deseeded, quartered and thinly sliced
125 g/4 oz smoked cod
salt and freshly ground black pepper

25 g/1 oz butter, melted
1 tbsp double cream
6 medium eggs, beaten

2 tbsp freshly chopped flat-leaf parsley
50 g/2 oz mature Cheddar cheese, grated

To serve:
crusty bread
tossed green salad, to serve

Heat the oil in a large, non-stick, heavy-based frying pan, add the potatoes, onions and garlic and cook gently for 10–15 minutes until golden brown, then add the red pepper and cook for 3 minutes.

Meanwhile, place the fish in a shallow frying pan and cover with water. Season to taste with salt and pepper and poach gently for 10 minutes. Drain and flake the fish into a bowl, toss in the melted butter and cream, adjust the seasoning and reserve.

When the vegetables are cooked, drain off any excess oil and stir in the beaten egg with the chopped parsley. Pour the fish mixture over the top and cook gently for 5 minutes, or until the eggs become firm.

Sprinkle the grated cheese over the top and place the pan under a preheated hot grill. Cook for 2–3 minutes until the cheese is golden and bubbling. Carefully slide the omelette onto a large plate and serve immediately with plenty of bread and salad.

Try this: FOR AN ALTERNATIVE: 286 FOR ENTERTAINING: 284

Supreme Baked Potatoes

SERVES 4

4 large baking potatoes
40 g/1½ oz butter
1 tbsp sunflower oil
1 carrot, peeled and
    chopped

2 celery stalks, trimmed and
    finely chopped
200 g can white crab meat
2 spring onions, trimmed
    and finely chopped

salt and freshly ground
    black pepper
50 g/2 oz Cheddar
    cheese, grated
tomato salad, to serve

Preheat the oven to 200°C/400°F/Gas Mark 6. Scrub the potatoes and prick all over with a fork, or thread two potatoes onto two long metal skewers. Place the potatoes in the preheated oven for 1–1½ hours, or until soft to the touch. Allow to cool a little, then cut in half.

Scoop out the cooked potato and turn into a bowl, leaving a reasonably firm potato shell. Mash the cooked potato flesh, then mix in the butter and mash until the butter has melted.

While the potatoes are cooking, heat the oil in a frying pan and cook the carrot and celery for 2 minutes. Cover the pan tightly and continue to cook for another 5 minutes, or until the vegetables are tender.

Add the cooked vegetables to the bowl of mashed potato and mix well. Fold in the crab meat and the spring onions, then season to taste with salt and pepper.

Pile the mixture back into the potato shells and press in firmly. Sprinkle the grated cheese over the top and return the potato halves to the oven for 12–15 minutes until hot, golden and bubbling. Serve immediately with a tomato salad.

Try this: FOR AN ALTERNATIVE: 74 FOR ENTERTAINING: 120

Smoked Mackerel & Potato Salad

SERVES 4

½ tsp dry mustard powder
1 large egg yolk
salt and freshly ground
    black pepper
150 ml/¼ pint sunflower oil
1–2 tbsp lemon juice

450 g/1 lb baby new
    potatoes
25 g/1 oz butter
350 g/12 oz smoked
    mackerel fillets
4 celery stalks, trimmed and

    finely chopped
3 tbsp creamed horseradish
150 ml/¼ pint crème fraîche
1 Little Gem, rinsed and
    roughly torn
8 cherry tomatoes, halved

Place the mustard powder and egg yolk in a small bowl with salt and pepper and whisk until blended. Add the oil, drop by drop, into the egg mixture, whisking continuously. When the mayonnaise is thick, add the lemon juice, drop by drop, until a smooth, glossy consistency is formed. Reserve.

Cook the potatoes in boiling salted water until tender, then drain. Cool slightly, then cut into halves or quarters, depending on size. Return to the saucepan and toss in the butter.

Remove the skin from the mackerel fillets and flake into pieces. Add to the potatoes in the saucepan, together with the celery.

Blend 4 tablespoons of the mayonnaise with the horseradish and crème fraîche. Season to taste with salt and pepper, then add to the potato and mackerel mixture and stir lightly.

Arrange the lettuce and tomatoes on four serving plates. Pile the smoked mackerel mixture on top of the lettuce, grind over a little pepper and serve with the remaining mayonnaise.

Try this: FOR AN ALTERNATIVE: 324   FOR ENTERTAINING: 252

Cheesy Vegetable & Prawn Bake

SERVES 4

175 g/6 oz long-grain rice
salt and freshly ground
   black pepper
1 garlic clove, peeled
   and crushed
1 large egg, beaten
3 tbsp freshly shredded basil

4 tbsp Parmesan
   cheese, grated
125 g/4 oz baby asparagus
   spears, trimmed
150 g/5 oz baby carrots,
   trimmed
150 g/5 oz fine green

beans, trimmed
150 g/5 oz cherry tomatoes
175 g/6 oz peeled prawns,
   thawed if frozen
125 g/4 oz mozzarella
   cheese, thinly sliced

Preheat the oven to 200°C/400°F/Gas Mark 6, about 10 minutes before required. Cook the rice in lightly salted boiling water for 12–15 minutes, or until tender, drain.

Stir in the garlic, beaten egg, shredded basil, 2 tablespoons of the Parmesan cheese and season to taste with salt and pepper. Press this mixture into a greased 23 cm/9 inch square ovenproof dish and reserve.

Bring a large saucepan of water to the boil, then drop in the asparagus, carrots and green beans. Return to the boil and cook for 3–4 minutes. Drain and leave to cool.

Quarter or halve the cherry tomatoes and mix them into the cooled vegetables. Spread the prepared vegetables over the rice and top with the prawns. Season to taste with salt and pepper.

Cover the prawns with the mozzarella and sprinkle over the remaining Parmesan cheese. Bake in the preheated oven for 20–25 minutes until piping hot and golden brown in places. Serve immediately.

Try this: FOR AN ALTERNATIVE: 270 FOR ENTERTAINING: 322

Fish Crumble

SERVES 6

450 g/1 lb whiting or
   halibut fillets
300 ml/½ pint milk
salt and freshly ground black
   pepper
1 tbsp sunflower oil
75 g/3 oz butter or
   margarine
1 medium onion, peeled and
   finely chopped

2 leeks, trimmed and sliced
1 medium carrot, peeled and
   cut into small dice
2 medium potatoes, peeled
   and cut into small pieces
175 g/6 oz plain flour
300 ml/½ pint fish or
   vegetable stock
2 tbsp whipping cream
1 tsp freshly chopped dill

runner beans, to serve

For the crumble topping:
75 g/3 oz butter or
   margarine
175 g/6 oz plain flour
75 g/3 oz Parmesan
   cheese, grated
¾ tsp cayenne pepper

Preheat the oven to 200°C/400°F/Gas Mark 6, 15 minutes before cooking. Oil a 1.4 litre/2½ pint pie dish. Place the fish in a saucepan with the milk, salt and pepper. Bring to the boil, cover and simmer for 8–10 minutes until the fish is cooked. Remove with a slotted spoon, reserving the cooking liquid. Flake the fish into the prepared dish.

Heat the oil and 1 tablespoon of the butter or margarine in a small frying pan and gently fry the onion, leeks, carrot and potatoes for 1–2 minutes. Cover tightly and cook over a gentle heat for a further 10 minutes until softened. Spoon the vegetables over the fish.

Melt the remaining butter or margarine in a saucepan, add the flour and cook for 1 minute, stirring. Whisk in the reserved cooking liquid and the stock. Cook until thickened, then stir in the cream. Remove from the heat and stir in the dill. Pour over the fish.

To make the crumble, rub the butter or margarine into the flour until it resembles bread-crumbs, then stir in the cheese and cayenne pepper. Sprinkle over the dish, and bake in the preheated oven for 20 minutes until piping hot. Serve with runner beans.

Try this: FOR AN ALTERNATIVE: 34   FOR ENTERTAINING: 90

Curly Endive & Seafood Salad

SERVES 4

1 head of curly endive
lettuce
2 green peppers
12.5 cm/5 inch piece
cucumber
125 g/4 oz squid, cleaned
and cut into thin rings
225 g/8 oz baby
asparagus spears

125 g/4 oz smoked salmon
slices, cut into wide strips
175 g/6 oz fresh cooked
mussels in their shells

For the lemon dressing:
2 tbsp sunflower oil
1 tbsp white wine vinegar
5 tbsp fresh lemon juice

1–2 tsp caster sugar
1 tsp mild wholegrain
mustard
salt and freshly ground
black pepper

To garnish:
slices of lemon
sprigs of fresh coriander

Rinse and tear the endive into small pieces and arrange on a serving platter. Remove the seeds from the peppers and cut the peppers and the cucumber into small dice. Sprinkle over the endive.

Bring a saucepan of water to the boil and add the squid rings. Bring the pan up to the boil again, then switch off the heat and leave it to stand for 5 minutes. Then drain and rinse thoroughly in cold water.

Cook the asparagus in boiling water for 5 minutes or until tender but just crisp. Arrange with the squid, smoked salmon and mussels on top of the salad.

To make the lemon dressing, put all the ingredients into a screw-topped jar or into a small bowl and mix thoroughly until the ingredients are combined.

Spoon 3 tablespoons of the dressing over the salad and serve the remainder in a small jug. Garnish the salad with slices of lemon and sprigs of coriander and serve.

Try this: FOR AN ALTERNATIVE: 18   FOR ENTERTAINING: 32

Mediterranean Feast

SERVES 4

1 small iceberg lettuce
225 g/8 oz French beans
225 g/8 oz baby new
    potatoes, scrubbed
4 medium eggs
1 green pepper
1 medium onion, peeled
200 g can tuna in brine,
    drained and flaked into
    small pieces

50 g/2 oz hard cheese,
    such as Edam, cut
    into small cubes
8 ripe but firm cherry
    tomatoes, quartered
50 g/2 oz black pitted
    olives, halved
freshly chopped basil,
    to garnish

For the lime vinaigrette:
3 tbsp light olive oil
2 tbsp white wine vinegar
4 tbsp lime juice
grated rind of 1 lime
1 tsp Dijon mustard
1-2 tsp caster sugar
salt and freshly ground
    black pepper

Cut the lettuce into four and remove the hard core. Tear into bite-sized pieces and arrange on a large serving platter or four individual plates. Cook the French beans in boiling salted water for 8 minutes and the potatoes for 10 minutes or until tender. Drain and rinse in cold water until cool, then cut both the beans and potatoes in half with a sharp knife.

Boil the eggs for 10 minutes, then rinse thoroughly under a cold running tap until cool. Remove the shells under water and cut each egg into four. Remove the seeds from the pepper and cut into thin strips and finely chop the onion.

Arrange the beans, potatoes, eggs, peppers and onion on top of the lettuce. Add the tuna, cheese and tomatoes. Sprinkle over the olives and garnish with the basil.

To make the vinaigrette, place all the ingredients in a screw-topped jar and shake vigorously until everything is mixed thoroughly. Spoon 4 tablespoons over the top of the prepared salad and serve the remainder separately.

Warm Lobster Salad with Hot Thai Dressing

SERVES 4

1 orange
50 g/2 oz granulated sugar
2 Cos lettuce hearts,
    shredded
1 small avocado, peeled and
    thinly sliced
½ cucumber, peeled,
    deseeded and thinly
    sliced
1 ripe mango, peeled,
    stoned and thinly sliced
1 tbsp butter or vegetable oil
1 large lobster, meat

removed and cut into
    bite-sized pieces
2 tbsp Thai or Italian
    basil leaves
4 large cooked prawns,
    peeled with tails left on,
    to garnish

For the dressing:
1 tbsp vegetable oil
4–6 spring onions, trimmed
    and sliced diagonally into
    5 cm/2 inch pieces

2.5 cm/1 inch piece fresh
    root ginger,
    peeled and grated
1 garlic clove,
    peeled and crushed
grated zest of 1 lime
juice of 2–3 small limes
2 tbsp Thai fish sauce
1 tbsp brown sugar
1–2 tsp sweet chilli sauce,
    or to taste
1 tbsp sesame oil

With a sharp knife, cut the orange rind into thin julienne strips, then cook in boiling water for 2 minutes. Drain the orange strips, then plunge into cold running water, drain and return to the saucepan with the sugar and 1 cm/½ inch water. Simmer until soft, then add 1 tablespoon of cold water to stop cooking. Remove from the heat and reserve. Arrange the lettuce on four large plates and arrange the avocado, cucumber and mango slices over the lettuce.

Heat a wok or large frying pan, add the butter or oil and when hot, but not sizzling, add the lobster and stir-fry for 1–2 minutes or until heated through. Remove and drain on absorbent kitchen paper. To make the dressing, heat the vegetable oil in a wok, then add the spring onions, ginger and garlic and stir-fry for 1 minute. Add the lime zest, lime juice, fish sauce, sugar and chilli sauce. Stir until the sugar dissolves. Remove from the heat, add the sesame oil with the orange rind and liquor. Arrange the lobster meat over the salad and drizzle with dressing. Sprinkle with basil leaves, garnish with prawns and serve immediately.

Try this: FOR AN ALTERNATIVE: 32 FOR ENTERTAINING: 24

Salmon with Herbed Potatoes

SERVES 4

450 g/1 lb baby new
  potatoes
salt and freshly ground
  black pepper
4 salmon steaks, each
  weighing about 175 g/6 oz

1 carrot, peeled and cut into
  fine strips
175 g/6 oz asparagus
  spears, trimmed
175 g/6 oz sugar snap
  peas, trimmed

finely grated rind and juice
  of 1 lemon
25 g/1 oz butter
4 large sprigs of
  fresh parsley

Preheat the oven to 190°C/375°F/Gas Mark 5, about 10 minutes before required. Parboil the potatoes in lightly salted boiling water for 5–8 minutes until they are barely tender. Drain and reserve. Cut out four pieces of baking parchment paper, measuring 20.5 cm/8 inches square, and place on the work surface. Arrange the parboiled potatoes on top. Wipe the salmon steaks and place on top of the potatoes.

Place the carrot strips in a bowl with the asparagus spears, sugar snaps and grated lemon rind and juice. Season to taste with salt and pepper. Toss lightly together.

Divide the vegetables evenly between the salmon. Dot the top of each parcel with butter and a sprig of parsley.

To wrap a parcel, lift up two opposite sides of the paper and fold the edges together. Twist the paper at the other two ends to seal the parcel well. Repeat with the remaining parcels.

Place the parcels on a baking tray and bake in the preheated oven for 15 minutes. Place an unopened parcel on each plate and open just before eating.

Try this: FOR AN ALTERNATIVE: 46 FOR ENTERTAINING: 64

Fresh Tuna Salad

SERVES 4

225 g/8 oz mixed
  salad leaves
225 g/8 oz baby cherry
  tomatoes, halved
  lengthways
125 g/4 oz rocket
  leaves, washed

2 tbsp groundnut oil
550 g/1¼ lb boned tuna
  steaks, each cut into 4
  small pieces
50 g/2 oz piece fresh
  Parmesan cheese

For the dressing:
8 tbsp olive oil
grated zest and juice of
  2 small lemons
1 tbsp wholegrain mustard
salt and freshly ground
  black pepper

Wash the salad leaves and place in a large salad bowl with the cherry tomatoes and rocket and reserve.

Heat the wok, then add the oil and heat until almost smoking. Add the tuna, skin-side down, and cook for 4–6 minutes, turning once during cooking, or until cooked and the flesh flakes easily. Remove from the heat and leave to stand in the juices for 2 minutes before removing.

Meanwhile make the dressing, place the olive oil, lemon zest and juices and mustard in a small bowl or screw-topped jar and whisk or shake well until well blended. Season to taste with salt and pepper.

Transfer the tuna to a clean chopping board and flake, then add it to the salad and toss lightly.

Using a swivel blade vegetable peeler, peel the piece of Parmesan cheese into shavings. Divide the salad between four large serving plates, drizzle the dressing over the salad, then scatter with the Parmesan shavings.

Try this: FOR AN ALTERNATIVE: 42   FOR ENTERTAINING: 24

Meat

Crispy Baked Potatoes with Serrano Ham

SERVES 4

4 large baking potatoes
4 tsp crème fraîche
salt and freshly ground
   black pepper
50 g/2 oz lean serrano ham
   or prosciutto, with fat

removed
50 g/2 oz cooked baby
   broad beans
50 g/2 oz cooked
   carrots, diced
50 g/2 oz cooked peas

50 g/2 oz hard cheese
   such as Edam or
   Cheddar, grated
fresh green salad,
   to serve

Preheat the oven to 200°C/400°F/Gas Mark 6. Scrub the potatoes dry. Prick with a fork and place on a baking sheet. Cook for 1–1½ hours or until tender when squeezed. Use oven gloves or a kitchen towel to pick up the potatoes as they will be very hot.

Cut the potatoes in half horizontally and scoop out all the flesh into a bowl. Spoon the crème fraîche into the bowl and mix thoroughly with the potatoes. Season to taste with a little salt and pepper.

Cut the ham into strips and carefully stir into the potato mixture with the broad beans, carrots and peas.

Pile the mixture back into the eight potato shells and sprinkle a little grated cheese on the top.

Place under a hot grill and cook until golden and heated through. Serve immediately with a fresh green salad.

Try this: FOR AN ALTERNATIVE: 40   FOR ENTERTAINING: 74

Oven–roasted Vegetables with Sausages

SERVES 4

2 medium aubergines,
    trimmed
3 medium courgettes,
    trimmed
4 tbsp olive oil
6 garlic cloves

8 Tuscany-style sausages
4 plum tomatoes
2 x 300 g cans
    cannellini beans
salt and freshly ground
    black pepper

1 bunch of fresh basil, torn
    into coarse pieces
4 tbsp Parmesan cheese,
    grated

Preheat the oven to 200°C/400°F/Gas Mark 6, 15 minutes before cooking. Cut the aubergines and courgettes into bite-sized chunks. Place the olive oil in a large roasting tin and heat in the preheated oven for 3 minutes, or until very hot. Add the aubergines, courgettes and garlic cloves, then stir until coated in the hot oil and cook in the oven for 10 minutes.

Remove the roasting tin from the oven and stir. Lightly prick the sausages, add to the roasting tin and return to the oven. Continue to roast for a further 20 minutes, turning once during cooking, until the vegetables are tender and the sausages are golden brown.

Meanwhile, roughly chop the plum tomatoes and drain the cannellini beans. Remove the sausages from the oven and stir in the tomatoes and cannellini beans. Season to taste with salt and pepper, then return to the oven for 5 minutes, or until heated thoroughly.

Scatter over the basil leaves and sprinkle with plenty of Parmesan cheese and extra freshly ground black pepper. Serve immediately.

Try this: FOR AN ALTERNATIVE: 34   FOR ENTERTAINING: 90

Pork Meatballs with Vegetables

SERVES 4

450 g/1 lb pork mince
2 tbsp freshly chopped
   coriander
2 garlic cloves,
   peeled and chopped
1 tbsp light soy sauce
salt and freshly ground
   black pepper
2 tbsp groundnut oil

2 cm/1 inch piece fresh root
   ginger, peeled and cut
   into matchsticks
1 red pepper, deseeded and
   cut into chunks
1 green pepper, deseeded
   and cut into chunks
2 courgettes, trimmed and
   cut into sticks

125 g/4 oz baby sweetcorn,
   halved lengthways
3 tbsp light soy sauce
1 tsp sesame oil
fresh coriander leaves,
   to garnish
freshly cooked noodles,
   to serve

Mix together the pork mince, the chopped coriander, half the garlic and the soy sauce, then season to taste with salt and pepper. Divide into 20 portions and roll into balls. Place on a baking sheet, cover with clingfilm and chill in the refrigerator for at least 30 minutes.

Heat a wok or large frying pan, add the groundnut oil and when hot, add the meatballs and cook for 8–10 minutes, or until the pork balls are browned all over, turning occasionally. Using a slotted spoon, transfer the balls to a plate and keep warm.

Add the ginger and remaining garlic to the wok and stir-fry for 30 seconds. Add the red and green peppers and stir-fry for 5 minutes. Add the courgettes and sweetcorn and stir-fry for 3 minutes.

Return the pork balls to the wok, add the soy sauce and sesame oil and stir-fry for 1 minute, until heated through. Garnish with coriander leaves and serve on a bed of noodles.

Try this: FOR AN ALTERNATIVE: 122   FOR ENTERTAINING: 280

Speedy Pork with Yellow Bean Sauce

SERVES 4

450 g/1 lb pork fillet
2 tbsp light soy sauce
2 tbsp orange juice
2 tsp cornflour
3 tbsp groundnut oil
2 garlic cloves, peeled

and crushed
175 g/6 oz carrots, peeled
and cut into matchsticks
125 g/4 oz fine green beans,
trimmed and halved
2 spring onions, trimmed

and cut into strips
4 tbsp yellow bean sauce
1 tbsp freshly chopped flat
leaf parsley, to garnish
freshly cooked egg noodles,
to serve

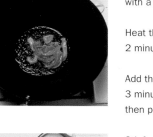

Remove any fat or sinew from the pork fillet, and cut into thin strips. Blend the soy sauce, orange juice and cornflour in a bowl and mix thoroughly. Place the meat in a shallow dish, pour over the soy sauce mixture, cover and leave to marinate in the refrigerator for 1 hour. Drain with a slotted spoon, reserving the marinade.

Heat the wok, then add 2 tablespoons of the oil and stir-fry the pork with the garlic for 2 minutes, or until the meat is sealed. Remove with a slotted spoon and reserve.

Add the remaining oil to the wok and cook the carrots, beans and spring onions for about 3 minutes, until tender but still crisp. Return the pork to the wok with the reserved marinade, then pour over the yellow bean sauce.

Stir-fry for a further 1–2 minutes, or until the pork is tender. Sprinkle with the chopped parsley and serve immediately with freshly cooked egg noodles.

Try this: FOR AN ALTERNATIVE: 76   FOR ENTERTAINING: 84

Hot Salami & Vegetable Gratin

SERVES 4

350 g/12 oz carrots
175 g/6 oz fine green beans
250 g/9 oz asparagus tips
175 g/6 oz frozen peas
225 g/8 oz Italian salami
1 tbsp olive oil

1 tbsp freshly chopped mint
25 g/1 oz butter
150 g/5 oz baby
  spinach leaves
150 ml/¼ pint double cream
salt and freshly ground

black pepper
1 small or ½ an olive
  ciabatta loaf
75 g/3 oz Parmesan
  cheese, grated
green salad, to serve

Preheat the oven to 200°C/400°F/Gas Mark 6. Peel and slice the carrots, trim the beans and asparagus and reserve. Cook the carrots in a saucepan of lightly salted, boiling water for 5 minutes. Add the remaining vegetables, except the spinach, and cook for about a further 5 minutes, or until tender. Drain and place in an ovenproof dish.

Discard any skin from the outside of the salami, if necessary, then chop roughly. Heat the oil in a frying pan and fry the salami for 4–5 minutes, stirring occasionally, until golden. Using a slotted spoon, transfer the salami to the ovenproof dish and scatter over the mint.

Add the butter to the frying pan and cook the spinach for 1–2 minutes, or until just wilted. Stir in the double cream and season well with salt and pepper. Spoon the mixture over the vegetables.

Whizz the ciabatta loaf in a food processor to make breadcrumbs. Stir in the Parmesan cheese and sprinkle over the vegetables. Bake in the preheated oven for 20 minutes, until golden and heated through. Serve with a green salad.

Try this: FOR AN ALTERNATIVE: 44   FOR ENTERTAINING: 322

Pork with Assorted Peppers

SERVES 4

450 g/1 lb pork fillet
2 tbsp groundnut oil
1 onion, peeled and
   thinly sliced
1 red pepper, deseeded
   and cut into strips
1 yellow pepper, deseeded
   and cut into strips

1 orange pepper, deseeded
   and cut into strips
2 garlic cloves, peeled
   and crushed
2 tsp paprika
400 g can chopped tomatoes
300 ml/½ pint pork or
   chicken stock

1 tsp soft dark brown sugar
salt and freshly ground
   black pepper
handful fresh
   oregano leaves
350 g/12 oz penne
2 tbsp grated mozzarella
   cheese

Trim the pork fillet, discarding any sinew and fat, then cut into small cubes. Heat the wok, add the oil and, when hot, stir-fry the pork for 3–4 minutes until they are brown and sealed. Remove the pork from the wok and reserve.

Add the sliced onions to the wok and stir-fry until they are softened, but not browned, then add the pepper strips and stir-fry for a further 3–4 minutes.

Stir in the garlic, paprika, chopped tomatoes, stock, sugar and seasoning and bring to the boil. Simmer, uncovered, stirring occasionally, for 15 minutes, or until the sauce has reduced and thickened. Return the pork to the wok and simmer for a further 5–10 minutes. Sprinkle with the oregano leaves.

Cook the pasta for 3–4 minutes until 'al dente' or according to packet directions, then drain and serve immediately with the pork and grated mozzarella cheese.

Try this: FOR AN ALTERNATIVE: 108   FOR ENTERTAINING: 290

Antipasto Penne

SERVES 4

3 medium courgettes,
   trimmed
4 plum tomatoes
175 g/6 oz Italian ham
2 tbsp olive oil
salt and freshly ground

black pepper
350 g/12 oz dried
   penne pasta
285 g jar antipasto
125 g/4 oz mozzarella
   cheese, drained and diced

125 g/4 oz Gorgonzola
   cheese, crumbled
3 tbsp freshly chopped
   flat-leaf parsley

Preheat the grill just before cooking. Cut the courgettes into thick slices. Rinse the tomatoes and cut into quarters, then cut the ham into strips. Pour the oil into a baking dish and place under the grill for 2 minutes, or until almost smoking. Remove from the grill and stir in the courgettes. Return to the grill and cook for 8 minutes, stirring occasionally. Remove from the grill and add the tomatoes and cook for a further 3 minutes.

Add the ham to the baking dish and cook under the grill for 4 minutes, until all the vegetables are charred and the ham is brown. Season to taste with salt and pepper.

Meanwhile, plunge the pasta into a large saucepan of lightly salted, boiling water, return to a rolling boil, stir and cook for 8 minutes, or until 'al dente'. Drain well and return to the saucepan.

Stir the antipasto into the vegetables and cook under the grill for 2 minutes, or until heated through. Add the cooked pasta and toss together gently with the remaining ingredients. Grill for a further 4 minutes, then serve immediately.

Try this: FOR AN ALTERNATIVE: 292 FOR ENTERTAINING: 258

Potato Skins

SERVES 4

4 large baking potatoes
2 tbsp olive oil
2 tsp paprika
125 g/4 oz pancetta,
   roughly chopped

6 tbsp double cream
125 g/4 oz Gorgonzola
   cheese
1 tbsp freshly
   chopped parsley

To serve:
mayonnaise
sweet chilli dipping sauce
tossed green salad

Preheat the oven to 200°C/400°F/Gas Mark 6. Scrub the potatoes, then prick a few times with a fork or skewer and place directly on the top shelf of the oven. Bake in the preheated oven for at least 1 hour, or until tender. The potatoes are cooked when they yield gently to the pressure of your hand.

Set the potatoes aside until cool enough to handle, then cut in half and scoop the flesh into a bowl and reserve. Preheat the grill and line the grill rack with tinfoil.

Mix together the oil and the paprika and use half to brush the outside of the potato skins. Place on the grill rack under the preheated hot grill and cook for 5 minutes, or until crisp, turning as necessary.

Heat the remaining paprika-flavoured oil and gently fry the pancetta until crisp. Add to the potato flesh along with the cream, Gorgonzola cheese and parsley. Halve the potato skins and fill with the Gorgonzola filling. Return to the oven for a further 15 minutes to heat through. Sprinkle with a little more paprika and serve immediately with mayonnaise, sweet chilli sauce and a green salad.

 Try this: FOR AN ALTERNATIVE: 274 FOR ENTERTAINING: 272

Pork with Spring Vegetables & Sweet Chilli Sauce

SERVES 4

450 g/16 oz pork fillet
2 tbsp sunflower oil
2 garlic cloves, peeled
    and crushed
2.5 cm/1 inch piece
    fresh root ginger,
    peeled and grated

125 g/4 oz carrots, peeled
    and cut into matchsticks
4 spring onions, trimmed
125 g/4 oz sugar snap peas
125 g/4 oz baby sweetcorn
2 tbsp sweet chilli sauce
2 tbsp light soy sauce

1 tbsp vinegar
½ tsp sugar, or to taste
125 g/4 oz beansprouts
grated zest of 1 orange
freshly cooked rice,
    to serve

Trim, then cut the pork fillet into thin strips and reserve. Heat a wok and pour in the oil. When hot, add the garlic and ginger and stir-fry for 30 seconds. Add the carrots to the wok and continue to stir-fry for 1–2 minute, or until they start to soften.

Slice the spring onions lengthways, then cut into three lengths. Trim the sugar snap peas and the sweetcorn. Add the spring onions, sugar snap peas and sweetcorn to the wok and stir-fry for 30 seconds.

Add the pork to the wok and continue to stir-fry for 2–3 minutes, or until the meat is sealed and browned all over. Blend the sweet chilli sauce, soy sauce, vinegar and sugar together, then stir into the wok with the beansprouts.

Continue to stir-fry until the meat is cooked and the vegetables are tender but still crisp. Sprinkle with the orange zest and serve immediately with the freshly cooked rice.

Try this: FOR AN ALTERNATIVE: 86 FOR ENTERTAINING: 96

Pork Cabbage Parcels

SERVES 4

8 large green
   cabbage leaves
1 tbsp vegetable oil
2 celery sticks, trimmed
   and chopped
1 carrot, peeled and cut
   into matchsticks
125 g/4 oz fresh pork mince
50 g/2 oz button

mushrooms, wiped
   and sliced
1 tsp Chinese five spice
   powder
50 g/2 oz cooked
   long-grain rice
juice of 1 lemon
1 tbsp soy sauce
150 ml/¼ pint chicken stock

For the tomato sauce:
1 tbsp vegetable oil
1 bunch spring onions,
   trimmed and chopped
400 g can chopped tomatoes
1 tbsp light soy sauce
1 tbsp freshly chopped mint
freshly ground black pepper

Preheat the oven to 180°C/350°F/Gas Mark 4, 10 minutes before cooking. To make the sauce, heat the oil in a heavy-based saucepan, add the spring onions and cook for 2 minutes or until softened. Add the tomatoes, soy sauce and mint to the saucepan, bring to the boil, cover, then simmer for 10 minutes. Season to taste with pepper. Reheat when required.

Meanwhile, blanch the cabbage leaves in a large saucepan of lightly salted water for 3 minutes. Drain and refresh under cold running water. Pat dry with absorbent kitchen paper and reserve.

Heat the oil in a small saucepan, add the celery, carrot and pork mince and cook for 3 minutes. Add the mushrooms and cook for 3 minutes. Stir in the Chinese five spice powder, rice, lemon juice and soy sauce and heat through.

Place some of the filling in the centre of each cabbage leaf and fold to enclose the filling. Place in a shallow ovenproof dish, seam-side down. Pour over the stock and cook in the preheated oven for 30 minutes. Serve immediately with the reheated tomato sauce.

 Try this: FOR AN ALTERNATIVE: 234 FOR ENTERTAINING: 214

Chef's Rice Salad

SERVES 4

225 g/8 oz wild rice
1/2 cucumber
175 g/6 oz cherry tomatoes
6 spring onions, trimmed
5 tbsp extra virgin olive oil
2 tbsp balsamic vinegar
1 tsp Dijon mustard

1 tsp caster sugar
salt and freshly ground
 black pepper
125 g/4 oz rocket
125 g/4 oz back bacon
125 g/4 oz cooked chicken
 meat, finely diced

125 g/4 oz Emmenthal
 cheese, grated
125 g/4 oz large cooked
 prawns, peeled
1 avocado, stoned, peeled
 and sliced, to garnish
warm crusty bread, to serve

Put the rice in in a saucepan of water and bring to the boil, stirring once or twice. Reduce the heat, cover and simmer gently for 30–50 minutes, depending on the texture you prefer. Drain well and reserve.

Thinly peel the cucumber, cut in half, then using a teaspoon, remove the seeds. Cut the cucumber into thin slices. Cut the tomatoes in quarters. Cut the spring onions into diagonal slices.

Whisk the olive oil with the vinegar, then whisk in the mustard and sugar. Season to taste with salt and pepper.

In a large bowl, gently toss together the cooled rice with the tomatoes, cucumber, spring onions and the rocket. Pour over the dressing and toss lightly together.

Heat a griddle pan and when hot cook the bacon on both sides for 4–6 minutes, or until crisp. Remove and chop. Arrange the prepared rocket salad on a platter, then arrange the bacon, chicken, cheese and prawns on top. Toss, if wished. Garnish with avocado slices and serve with plenty of warm, crusty bread.

Try this: FOR AN ALTERNATIVE: 22 FOR ENTERTAINING: 112

Special Rosti

SERVES 4

700 g/1½ lb potatoes, scrubbed but not peeled
salt and freshly ground black pepper
75 g/3 oz butter
1 large onion, peeled and finely chopped

1 garlic clove, peeled and crushed
2 tbsp freshly chopped parsley
1 tbsp olive oil
75 g/3 oz Parma ham, thinly sliced

50 g/2 oz sun-dried tomatoes, chopped
175 g/ 6 oz Emmenthal cheese, grated
mixed green salad, to serve

Cook the potatoes in a large saucepan of salted boiling water for about 10 minutes, until just tender. Drain in a colander, then rinse in cold water. Drain again. Leave until cool enough to handle, then peel off the skins.

Melt the butter in a large frying pan and gently fry the onion and garlic for about 3 minutes until softened and beginning to colour. Remove from the heat.

Coarsely grate the potatoes into a large bowl, then stir in the onion and garlic mixture. Sprinkle over the parsley and stir well to mix. Season to taste with salt and pepper.

Heat the oil in the frying pan and cover the base of the pan with half the potato mixture. Lay the slices of Parma ham on top. Sprinkle with the chopped sun-dried tomatoes, then scatter the grated Emmenthal over the top.

Finally, top with the remaining potato mixture. Cook over a low heat, pressing down with a palette knife from time to time, for 10–15 minutes, or until the bottom is golden brown. Carefully invert the rosti onto a large plate, then carefully slide back into the pan and cook the other side until golden. Serve cut into wedges with a mixed green salad.

Try this: FOR AN ALTERNATIVE: 74 FOR ENTERTAINING: 176

Beef & Baby Corn Stir Fry

SERVES 4

3 tbsp light soy sauce
1 tbsp clear honey, warmed
450 g/1 lb beef rump steak,
    trimmed and thinly sliced
6 tbsp groundnut oil
125 g/4 oz shiitake
    mushrooms,
    wiped and halved
125 g/4 oz beansprouts,
    rinsed

2.5 cm/1 inch piece fresh
    root ginger, peeled and
    cut into matchsticks
125 g/4 oz mangetout,
    halved lengthways
125 g/4 oz broccoli, trimmed
    and cut into florets
1 medium carrot, peeled and
    cut into matchsticks
125 g/4 oz baby sweetcorn

cobs, halved lengthways
¼ head Chinese leaves,
    shredded
1 tbsp chilli sauce
3 tbsp black bean sauce
1 tbsp dry sherry
freshly cooked noodles,
    to serve

Mix together the soy sauce and honey in a shallow dish. Add the sliced beef and turn to coat evenly. Cover with clingfilm and leave to marinate for at least 30 minutes, turning occasionally.

Heat a wok or large frying pan, add 2 tablespoons of the oil and heat until just smoking. Add the mushrooms and stir-fry for 1 minute. Add the bean sprouts and stir-fry for 1 minute. Using a slotted spoon, transfer the mushroom mixture to a plate and keep warm.

Drain the beef, reserving the marinade. Reheat the wok, pour in 2 tablespoons of the oil and heat until smoking. Add the beef and stir-fry for 4 minutes or until browned. Transfer to a plate and keep warm.

Add the remaining oil to the wok and heat until just smoking. Add the ginger, mangetout, broccoli, carrot and the baby sweetcorn with the shredded Chinese leaves and stir-fry for 3 minutes. Stir in the chilli and black bean sauces, the sherry, the reserved marinade and the beef and mushroom mixture. Stir-fry for 2 minutes, then serve immediately with freshly cooked noodles.

Try this: FOR AN ALTERNATIVE: 348   FOR ENTERTAINING: 76

Sweet & Sour Shredded Beef

SERVES 4

350 g/12 oz rump steak
1 tsp sesame oil
2 tbsp Chinese rice wine or
    sweet sherry
2 tbsp dark soy sauce
1 tsp cornflour
4 tbsp pineapple juice
2 tsp soft light brown sugar

1 tsp sherry vinegar
salt and freshly ground
    black pepper
2 tbsp groundnut oil
2 medium carrots, peeled
    and cut into matchsticks
125 g/4 oz mangetout peas,
    trimmed and cut into

matchsticks
1 bunch spring onions,
    trimmed and shredded
2 garlic cloves, peeled
    and crushed
1 tbsp toasted sesame seeds
freshly cooked Thai fragrant
    rice, to serve

Cut the steak across the grain into thin strips. Put in a bowl with the sesame oil, 1 tablespoon of the Chinese rice wine or sherry and 1 tablespoon of the soy sauce. Mix well, cover and leave to marinate in the refrigerator for 30 minutes.

In a small bowl, blend together the cornflour with the remaining Chinese rice wine or sherry, then stir in the pineapple juice, remaining soy sauce, sugar and vinegar. Season with a little salt and pepper and reserve.

Heat a wok until hot, add 1 tablespoon of the oil, then drain the beef, reserving the marinade, and stir-fry for 1–2 minutes, or until browned. Remove from the wok and reserve.

Add the remaining oil to the wok then add the carrots and stir-fry for 1 minute, then add the mangetout peas and spring onions and stir-fry for a further 1 minute.

Return the beef to the wok with the sauce, reserved marinade and garlic. Continue cooking for 1 minute or until the vegetables are tender and the sauce is bubbling. Turn the stir-fry into a warmed serving dish, sprinkle with toasted sesame seeds and serve immediately with the Thai fragrant rice.

Try this: FOR AN ALTERNATIVE: 84   FOR ENTERTAINING: 92

Spicy Lamb & Peppers

SERVES 4

550 g/1¼ lb lamb fillet
4 tbsp soy sauce
1 tbsp dry sherry
1 tbsp cornflour
3 tbsp vegetable oil
1 bunch spring onions,
　shredded
225 g/8 oz broccoli florets
2 garlic cloves, peeled

and chopped
2.5 cm/1 inch piece fresh
　root ginger, peeled and
　cut into matchsticks
1 red pepper, deseeded and
　cut into chunks
1 green pepper, deseeded
　and cut into chunks
2 tsp Chinese five spice

powder
1–2 tsp dried crushed
　chillies, or to taste
1 tbsp tomato purée
1 tbsp rice wine vinegar
1 tbsp soft brown sugar
freshly cooked noodles,
　to serve

Cut the lamb into 2 cm/¾ inch slices, then place in a shallow dish. Blend the soy sauce, sherry and cornflour together in a small bowl and pour over the lamb. Turn the lamb until coated lightly with the marinade. Cover with clingfilm and leave to marinate in the refrigerator for at least 30 minutes, turning occasionally.

Heat a wok or large frying pan, add the oil and when hot, stir-fry the spring onions and broccoli for 2 minutes. Add the garlic, ginger and peppers and stir-fry for a further 2 minutes. Using a slotted spoon, transfer the vegetables to a plate and keep warm.

Using a slotted spoon, lift the lamb from the marinade, shaking off any excess marinade. Add to the wok and stir-fry for 5 minutes, or until browned all over. Reserve the marinade.

Return the vegetables to the wok and stir in the Chinese five spice powder, chillies, tomato purée, reserved marinade, vinegar and sugar. Bring to the boil, stirring constantly, until thickened. Simmer for 2 minutes or until heated through thoroughly. Serve immediately with noodles.

　　Try this: FOR AN ALTERNATIVE: 92　FOR ENTERTAINING: 110

Lamb & Potato Moussaka

SERVES 4

700 g/1½ lb cooked roast lamb
700 g/1½ lb potatoes, peeled
125 g/4 oz butter
1 large onion, peeled and chopped
2–4 garlic cloves, peeled and crushed
3 tbsp tomato purée
1 tbsp freshly chopped parsley
salt and freshly ground black pepper
3–4 tbsp olive oil
2 medium aubergines, trimmed and sliced
4 medium tomatoes, sliced
2 medium eggs
300 ml/½ pint Greek yogurt
2–3 tbsp Parmesan cheese, grated

Preheat the oven to 200°C/400°F/Gas Mark 6, about 15 minutes before required. Trim the lamb, discarding any fat then cut into fine dice and reserve. Thinly slice the potatoes and rinse thoroughly in cold water, then pat dry with a clean tea towel.

Melt 50 g/2 oz of the butter in a frying pan and fry the potatoes, in batches, until crisp and golden. Using a slotted spoon, remove from the pan and reserve. Use a third of the potatoes to line the base of an ovenproof dish.

Add the onion and garlic to the butter remaining in the pan and cook for 5 minutes. Add the lamb and fry for 1 minute. Blend the tomato purée with 3 tablespoons of water and stir into the pan with the parsley and salt and pepper. Spoon over the layer of potatoes, then top with the remaining potato slices.

Heat the oil and the remaining butter in the pan and brown the aubergine slices for 5–6 minutes. Arrange the tomatoes on top of the potatoes, then the aubergines on top of the tomatoes. Beat the eggs with the yogurt and Parmesan cheese and pour over the aubergine and tomatoes. Bake in the preheated oven for 25 minutes, or until golden and piping hot. Serve.

Try this: FOR AN ALTERNATIVE: 46   FOR ENTERTAINING: 68

Lamb with Stir–fried Vegetables

SERVES 4

550 g/1¼ lb lamb fillet, cut into strips
2.5 cm/1 inch piece fresh root ginger, peeled and cut into matchsticks
2 garlic cloves, peeled and chopped
4 tbsp soy sauce
2 tbsp dry sherry

2 tsp cornflour
4 tbsp groundnut oil
75 g/3 oz French beans, trimmed and cut in half
2 medium carrots, peeled and cut into matchsticks
1 red pepper, deseeded and cut into chunks
1 yellow pepper, deseeded

and cut into chunks
225 g can water chestnuts, drained and halved
3 tomatoes, chopped
freshly cooked sticky rice in banana leaves, to serve (optional)

Place the lamb strips in a shallow dish. Mix together the ginger and half the garlic in a small bowl. Pour over the soy sauce and sherry and stir well. Pour over the lamb and stir until coated lightly. Cover with clingfilm and leave to marinate for at least 30 minutes, occasionally spooning the marinade over the lamb.

Using a slotted spoon, lift the lamb from the marinade and place on a plate. Blend the cornflour and the marinade together until smooth and reserve.

Heat a wok or large frying pan, add 2 tablespoons of the oil and when hot, add the remaining garlic, French beans, carrots and peppers and stir-fry for 5 minutes. Using a slotted spoon, transfer the vegetables to a plate and keep warm.

Heat the remaining oil in the wok, add the lamb and stir-fry for 2 minutes or until tender. Return the vegetables to the wok with the water chestnuts, tomatoes and reserved marinade mixture. Bring to the boil then simmer for 1 minute. Serve immediately with freshly cooked sticky rice in banana leaves, if liked.

Try this: FOR AN ALTERNATIVE: 76 FOR ENTERTAINING: 70

Poultry

Chicken & Baby Vegetable Stir Fry

SERVES 4

2 tbsp groundnut oil
1 small red chilli, deseeded
   and finely chopped
150 g/5 oz chicken breast
   or thigh meat, skinned
   and cut into cubes
2 baby leeks, trimmed
   and sliced
12 asparagus spears, halved

125 g/4 oz mangetout
   peas, trimmed
125 g/4 oz baby carrots,
   trimmed and halved
   lengthways
125 g/4 oz fine green beans,
   trimmed and
   diagonally sliced
125 g/4 oz baby sweetcorn,

   diagonally halved
50 ml/2 fl oz chicken stock
2 tsp light soy sauce
1 tbsp dry sherry
1 tsp sesame oil
toasted sesame seeds,
   to garnish

Heat the wok until very hot and add the oil. Add the chopped chilli and chicken and stir-fry for 4–5 minutes, or until the chicken is cooked and golden.

Increase the heat, add the leeks to the chicken and stir-fry for 2 minutes. Add the asparagus spears, mangetout peas, baby carrots, green beans, and baby sweetcorn. Stir-fry for 3–4 minutes, or until the vegetables soften slightly but still retain a slight crispness.

In a small bowl, mix together the chicken stock, soy sauce, dry sherry and sesame oil. Pour into the wok, stir and cook until heated through. Sprinkle with the toasted sesame seeds and serve immediately.

Try this: FOR AN ALTERNATIVE: 84   FOR ENTERTAINING: 106

Warm Fruity Rice Salad

SERVES 4

175 g/6 oz mixed basmati and wild rice
125 g/4 oz skinless chicken breast
300 ml/½ pint chicken or vegetable stock
125 g/4 oz ready-to-eat dried apricots

125 g/4 oz ready-to-eat dried dates
3 sticks celery

For the dressing:
2 tbsp sunflower oil
1 tbsp white wine vinegar
4 tbsp lemon juice

1–2 tsp clear honey, warmed
1 tsp Dijon mustard
freshly ground black pepper

To garnish:
6 spring onions
sprigs of fresh coriander

Place the rice in a pan of boiling salted water and cook for 15–20 minutes or until tender. Rinse thoroughly with boiling water and reserve.

Meanwhile wipe the chicken and place in a shallow saucepan with the stock. Bring to the boil, cover and simmer for about 15 minutes or until the chicken is cooked thoroughly and the juices run clear. Leave the chicken in the stock until cool enough to handle, then cut into thin slices.

Chop the apricots and dates into small pieces. Peel any tough membranes from the outside of the celery and chop into dice. Fold the apricots, dates, celery and sliced chicken into the warm rice.

Make the dressing by whisking all the ingredients together in a small bowl until mixed thoroughly. Pour 2–3 tablespoons over the rice and stir in gently and evenly. Serve the remaining dressing separately.

Trim and chop the spring onions. Sprinkle the spring onions over the top of the salad and garnish with the sprigs of coriander. Serve while still warm.

Try this: FOR AN ALTERNATIVE: 102   FOR ENTERTAINING: 114

Poached Chicken with Salsa Verde Herb Sauce

SERVES 6

6 boneless chicken breasts, each about 175 g/6 oz
600 ml/1 pint chicken stock, preferably homemade

For the salsa verde:
2 garlic cloves, peeled and chopped
4 tbsp freshly chopped parsley

3 tbsp freshly chopped mint
2 tsp capers
2 tbsp chopped gherkins (optional)
2–3 anchovy fillets in olive oil, drained and finely chopped (optional)
1 handful wild rocket leaves, chopped (optional)
2 tbsp lemon juice or red

wine vinegar
125 ml/4 fl oz extra virgin olive oil
salt and freshly ground black pepper
sprigs of mint, to garnish
freshly cooked vegetables, to serve

Place the chicken breasts with the stock in a large frying pan and bring to the boil. Reduce the heat and simmer for 10–15 minutes, or until cooked. Leave to cool in the stock.

To make the salsa verde, switch the motor on a food processor, then drop in the garlic cloves and chop finely. Add the parsley and mint and, using the pulse button, pulse 2–3 times. Add the capers and, if using, add the gherkins, anchovies and rocket. Pulse 2–3 times until the sauce is evenly textured.

With the machine still running, pour in the lemon juice or red wine vinegar, then add the olive oil in a slow, steady stream until the sauce is smooth. Season to taste with salt and pepper, then transfer to a large serving bowl and reserve.

Carve each chicken breast into thick slices and arrange on serving plates, fanning out the slices slightly. Spoon over a little of the salsa verde on to each chicken breast, garnish with sprigs of mint and serve immediately with freshly cooked vegetables.

Try this: FOR AN ALTERNATIVE: 66   FOR ENTERTAINING: 28

Chicken Satay Salad

SERVES 4

4 tbsp crunchy peanut butter
1 tbsp chilli sauce
1 garlic clove, peeled
   and crushed
2 tbsp cider vinegar
2 tbsp light soy sauce
2 tbsp dark soy sauce

2 tsp soft brown sugar
pinch of salt
2 tsp freshly ground
   Szechuan peppercorns
450 g/1 lb dried egg noodles
2 tbsp sesame oil
1 tbsp groundnut oil

450 g/1 lb skinless, boneless
   chicken breast fillets, cut
   into cubes
shredded celery leaves,
   to garnish
cos lettuce, to serve

Place the peanut butter, chilli sauce, garlic, cider vinegar, soy sauces, sugar, salt and ground peppercorns in a food processor and blend to form a smooth paste. Scrape into a bowl, cover and chill in the refrigerator until required.

Bring a large saucepan of lightly salted water to the boil. Add the noodles and cook for 3–5 minutes. Drain and plunge into cold water. Drain again and toss in the sesame oil. Leave to cool.

Heat the wok until very hot, add the oil and when hot, add the chicken cubes. Stir-fry for 5–6 minutes until the chicken is golden brown and cooked through.

Remove the chicken from the wok using a slotted spoon and add to the noodles, together with the peanut sauce. Mix lightly together, then sprinkle with the shredded celery leaves and either serve immediately or leave until cold, then serve with cos lettuce.

Try this: FOR AN ALTERNATIVE: 328   FOR ENTERTAINING: 116

Chicken & Pasta Salad

SERVES 6

450 g/1 lb short pasta
2–3 tbsp extra virgin olive oil
300 g/11 oz cold cooked
    chicken, cut into bite-sized
    pieces (preferably roasted)
1 red pepper, deseeded
    and diced
1 yellow pepper,
    deseeded and diced
4–5 sun-dried tomatoes,

sliced
2 tbsp capers, rinsed
    and drained
125 g/4 oz pitted Italian
    black olives
4 spring onions, chopped
225 g/8 oz mozzarella
    cheese, preferably
    buffalo, diced
salt and freshly ground

black pepper

For the dressing:
50 ml/2 fl oz red or white
    wine vinegar
1 tbsp mild mustard
1 tsp sugar
75–125 ml/ 3–4 fl oz
    extra virgin olive oil
125 ml/4 fl oz mayonnaise

Bring a large saucepan of lightly salted water to the boil. Add the pasta and cook for 10 minutes, or until 'al dente'. Drain the pasta and rinse under cold running water, then drain again. Place in a large serving bowl and toss with the olive oil.

Add the chicken, diced red and yellow peppers, sliced sun-dried tomatoes, capers, olives, spring onions and mozzarella to the pasta and toss gently until mixed. Season to taste with salt and pepper.

To make the dressing, put the vinegar, mustard and sugar into a small bowl or jug and whisk until well blended and the sugar is dissolved. Season with some pepper, then gradually whisk in the olive oil in a slow, steady stream until a thickened vinaigrette forms.

Put the mayonnaise in a bowl and gradually whisk in the dressing until smooth. Pour over the pasta mixture and mix gently until all the ingredients are coated. Turn into a large, shallow serving bowl and serve at room temperature.

   Try this: FOR AN ALTERNATIVE: 110 FOR ENTERTAINING: 298

Stir–fried Chicken with Spinach, Tomatoes & Pine Nuts

SERVES 4

50 g/2 oz pine nuts
2 tbsp sunflower oil
1 red onion, peeled and
   finely chopped
450 g/1 lb skinless, boneless
   chicken breast fillets, cut
   into strips

450 g/1 lb cherry
   tomatoes, halved
225 g/8 oz baby
   spinach, washed
salt and freshly ground
   black pepper
¼ tsp freshly grated nutmeg

2 tbsp balsamic vinegar
50 g/2 oz raisins
freshly cooked ribbon
   noodles tossed in butter,
   to serve

Heat the wok and add the pine nuts. Dry-fry for about 2 minutes, shaking often to ensure that they toast but do not burn. Remove and reserve. Wipe any dust from the wok.

Heat the wok again, add the oil and when hot, add the red onion and stir-fry for 2 minutes. Add the chicken and stir-fry for 2–3 minutes, or until golden brown. Reduce the heat, toss in the cherry tomatoes and stir-fry gently until the tomatoes start to disintegrate.

Add the baby spinach and stir-fry for 2–3 minutes, or until they start to wilt. Season to taste with salt and pepper, then sprinkle in the grated nutmeg and drizzle in the balsamic vinegar.

Finally, stir in the raisins and reserved toasted pine nuts. Serve immediately on a bed of buttered ribbon noodles.

Try this: FOR AN ALTERNATIVE: 88   FOR ENTERTAINING: 96

Mixed Vegetable & Chicken Pasta

SERVES 4

3 medium courgettes,
 trimmed
4 plum tomatoes
175 g/6 oz Italian ham
2 tbsp olive oil
salt and freshly ground

black pepper
350 g/12 oz dried
 penne pasta
285 g jar antipasto
125 g/4 oz mozzarella
 cheese, drained and diced

125 g/4 oz Gorgonzola
 cheese, crumbled
3 tbsp freshly chopped flat
 leaf parsley

Preheat the grill just before using. Cut the chicken into thin strips. Trim the leeks, leaving some of the dark green tops, then shred and wash thoroughly in plenty of cold water. Peel the onion and cut into thin wedges.

Bring a large pan of lightly salted water to a rolling boil. Add the pasta and cook according to the packet instructions, or until 'al dente'.

Meanwhile, melt butter with the olive oil in a large heavy-based pan, add the chicken and cook, stirring occasionally, for 8 minutes, or until browned all over. Add the leeks and onion and cook for 5 minutes, or until softened. Add the garlic and cherry tomatoes and cook for a further 2 minutes.

Stir the cream and asparagus tips into the chicken and vegetable mixture, bring to the boil slowly, then remove from the heat. Drain the pasta thoroughly and return to the pan. Pour the sauce over the pasta, season to taste with salt and pepper, then toss lightly.

Tip the pasta mixture into a gratin dish and sprinkle with the cheese. Cook under the preheated grill for 5 minutes, or until bubbling and golden, turning the dish occasionally. Serve immediately with a green salad.

Try this: FOR AN ALTERNATIVE: 44   FOR ENTERTAINING: 322

Pasta & Pepper Salad

SERVES 4

4 tbsp olive oil
1 each red, orange
   and yellow pepper,
   deseeded and cut
   into chunks
1 large courgette, trimmed
   and cut into chunks
1 medium aubergine,
   trimmed and diced

275 g/10 oz fusilli
4 plum tomatoes, quartered
1 bunch fresh basil leaves,
   roughly chopped
2 tbsp pesto
2 garlic cloves, peeled and
   roughly chopped
1 tbsp lemon juice
225 g/8 oz boneless and

skinless roasted
   chicken breast
salt and freshly ground
   black pepper
125 g/4 oz feta cheese,
   crumbled
crusty bread, to serve

Preheat the oven to 200°C/400°F/Gas Mark 6. Spoon the olive oil into a roasting tin and heat in the oven for 2 minutes, or until almost smoking. Remove from the oven, add the peppers, courgette and aubergine and stir until coated. Bake for 30 minutes, or until charred, stirring occasionally.

Bring a large pan of lightly salted water to a rolling boil. Add the pasta and cook according to the packet instructions, or until 'al dente'. Drain and refresh under cold running water. Drain thoroughly, place in a large salad bowl and reserve.

Remove the cooked vegetables from the oven and allow to cool. Add to the cooled pasta, together with the quartered tomatoes, chopped basil leaves, pesto, garlic and lemon juice. Toss lightly to mix.

Shred the chicken roughly into small pieces and stir into the pasta and vegetable mixture. Season to taste with salt and pepper, then sprinkle the crumbled feta cheese over the pasta and stir gently. Cover the dish and leave to marinate for 30 minutes, stirring occasionally. Serve the salad with fresh crusty bread.

Try this: FOR AN ALTERNATIVE: 104   FOR ENTERTAINING: 324

Spicy Chicken & Pasta Salad

SERVES 6

450 g/1 lb pasta shells
25 g/1 oz butter
1 onion, peeled and
    chopped
2 tbsp mild curry paste
125 g/4 oz ready-to-eat dried
    apricots, chopped

2 tbsp tomato paste
3 tbsp mango chutney
300 ml/½ pint mayonnaise
425 g can pineapple slices
    in fruit juice
salt and freshly ground
    black pepper

450 g/1 lb skinned and
    boned cooked chicken,
    cut into bite-sized pieces
25 g/1 oz flaked toasted
    almond slivers
coriander sprigs,
    to garnish

Bring a large pan of lightly salted water to a rolling boil. Add the pasta shells and cook according to the packet instructions, or until 'al dente'. Drain and refresh under cold running water then drain thoroughly and place in a large serving bowl.

Meanwhile, melt the butter in a heavy-based pan, add the onion and cook for 5 minutes, or until softened. Add the curry paste and cook, stirring, for 2 minutes. Stir in the apricots and tomato paste, then cook for 1 minute. Remove from the heat and allow to cool.

Blend the mango chutney and mayonnaise together in a small bowl. Drain the pineapple slices, adding 2 tablespoons of the pineapple juice to the mayonnaise mixture; reserve the pineapple slices. Season the mayonnaise to taste with salt and pepper.

Cut the pineapple slices into chunks and stir into the pasta together with the mayonnaise mixture, curry paste and cooked chicken pieces. Toss lightly together to coat the pasta. Sprinkle with the almond slivers, garnish with coriander sprigs and serve.

Try this: FOR AN ALTERNATIVE: 114   FOR ENTERTAINING: 312

Rice & Papaya Salad

SERVES 4

175 g/6 oz easy-cook
  basmati rice
1 cinnamon stick, bruised
1 bird's-eye chilli, deseeded
  and finely chopped
rind and juice of 2 limes
rind and juice of 2 lemons
2 tbsp Thai fish sauce

1 tbsp soft light brown sugar
1 papaya, peeled and
  seeds removed
1 mango, peeled and
  stone removed
1 green chilli, deseeded
  and finely chopped
2 tbsp freshly chopped

  coriander
1 tbsp freshly chopped mint
250 g/9 oz cooked chicken
50 g/2 oz roasted
  peanuts, chopped
strips of pitta bread,
  to serve

Rinse and drain the rice and pour into a saucepan. Add 450 ml/¾ pint boiling salted water and the cinnamon stick. Bring to the boil, reduce the heat to a very low heat, cover and cook without stirring for 15–18 minutes, or until all the liquid is absorbed. The rice should be light and fluffy and have steam holes on the surface. Remove the cinnamon stick and stir in the rind from 1 lime.

To make the dressing, place the bird's-eye chilli, remaining rind and lime and lemon juice, fish sauce and sugar in a food processor, mix for a few minutes until blended. Alternatively, place all these ingredients in a screw-top jar and shake until well blended. Pour half the dressing over the hot rice and toss until the rice glistens.

Slice the papaya and mango into thin slices, then place in a bowl. Add the chopped green chilli, coriander and mint. Place the chicken on a chopping board, then remove and discard any skin or sinews. Cut into fine shreds and add to the bowl with the chopped peanuts.

Add the remaining dressing to the chicken mixture and stir until all the ingredients are lightly coated. Spoon the rice onto a platter, pile the chicken mixture on top and serve with warm strips of pitta bread.

Try this: FOR AN ALTERNATIVE: 98   FOR ENTERTAINING: 120

Wild Rice & Bacon Salad with Smoked Chicken

SERVES 4

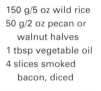

150 g/5 oz wild rice
50 g/2 oz pecan or
   walnut halves
1 tbsp vegetable oil
4 slices smoked
   bacon, diced

3–4 shallots, peeled and
   finely chopped
75 ml/3 fl oz walnut oil
2–3 tbsp sherry or
   cider vinegar
2 tbsp freshly chopped dill

salt and freshly ground
   black pepper
275 g/10 oz smoked
   chicken or duck
   breast, thinly sliced
dill sprigs, to garnish

Put the wild rice in a medium saucepan with 600 ml/1 pint water and bring to the boil, stirring once or twice. Reduce the heat, cover and simmer gently for 30–50 minutes, depending on the texture you prefer, chewy or tender. Using a fork, gently fluff into a large bowl and leave to cool slightly.

Meanwhile, toast the nuts in a frying pan over a medium heat for 2 minutes, or until they are fragrant and lightly coloured, stirring and tossing frequently. Cool, then chop coarsely and add to the rice.

Heat the oil in the frying pan over a medium heat. Add the bacon and cook, stirring from time to time, for 3–4 minutes, or until crisp and brown. Remove from the pan and drain on absorbent kitchen paper. Add the shallots to the pan and cook for 4 minutes, or until just softened, stirring from time to time. Stir into the rice and nuts, with the drained bacon pieces.

Whisk the walnut oil, vinegar, half the dill and salt and pepper in a small bowl until combined. Pour the dressing over the rice mixture and toss well to combine. Mix the chicken and the remaining chopped dill into the rice, then spoon into bowls and garnish each serving with a dill sprig. Serve slightly warm, or at room temperature.

Try this: FOR AN ALTERNATIVE: 120   FOR ENTERTAINING: 134

Chicken Pie with Sweet Potato Topping

SERVES 4

700 g/1½ lb sweet potatoes, peeled and cut into chunks
salt and freshly ground black pepper
250 g/9 oz potatoes, peeled and cut into chunks
150 ml/¼ pint milk
25 g/1 oz butter

2 tsp brown sugar
grated rind of 1 orange
4 skinless chicken breast fillets, diced
1 medium onion, peeled and coarsely chopped
125 g/4 oz baby mushrooms, stems trimmed
2 leeks, trimmed and

thickly sliced
150 ml/¼ pint dry white wine
1 chicken stock cube
1 tbsp freshly chopped parsley
50 ml/2 fl oz crème fraîche or thick double cream
green vegetables, to serve

Preheat the oven to 190°C/375°F/Gas Mark 5, 10 minutes before required. Cook the potatoes in lightly salted boiling water until tender. Drain well, then return to the saucepan and mash until smooth and creamy, gradually adding the milk, then the butter, sugar and orange rind. Season to taste with salt and pepper and reserve.

Place the chicken in a saucepan with the onion, mushrooms, leeks, wine, stock cube and season to taste. Simmer, covered, until the chicken and vegetables are tender. Using a slotted spoon, transfer the chicken and vegetables to a 1.1 litre/2 pint pie dish. Add the parsley and crème fraîche or cream to the liquid in the pan and bring to the boil. Simmer until thickened and smooth, stirring constantly. Pour over the chicken in the pie dish, mix and cool.

Spread the mashed potato over the chicken filling, and swirl the surface into decorative peaks. Bake in the preheated oven for 35 minutes, or until the top is golden and the chicken filling is heated through. Serve immediately with fresh green vegetables.

Try this: FOR AN ALTERNATIVE: 46   FOR ENTERTAINING: 90

Warm Chicken & Potato Salad with Peas & Mint

SERVES 4-6

450 g/1 lb new potatoes, peeled or scrubbed and cut into bite-sized pieces
salt and freshly ground black pepper
2 tbsp cider vinegar
175 g/6 oz frozen garden peas, thawed

1 small ripe avocado
4 cooked chicken breasts, about 450 g/1 lb in weight, skinned and diced
2 tbsp freshly chopped mint
2 heads Little Gem lettuce
fresh mint sprigs, to garnish

For the dressing:
2 tbsp raspberry or sherry vinegar
2 tsp Dijon mustard
1 tsp clear honey
50 ml/2 fl oz sunflower oil
50 ml/2 fl oz extra virgin olive oil

Cook the potatoes in lightly salted boiling water for 15 minutes, or until just tender when pierced with the tip of a sharp knife; do not overcook. Rinse under cold running water to cool slightly, then drain and turn into a large bowl. Sprinkle with the cider vinegar and toss gently.

Run the peas under hot water to ensure that they are thawed, pat dry with absorbent kitchen paper and add to the potatoes.

Cut the avocado in half lengthways and remove the stone. Peel and cut the avocado into cubes and add to the potatoes and peas. Add the chicken and stir together lightly.

To make the dressing, place all the ingredients in a screw-top jar, with a little salt and pepper and shake well to mix – add a little more oil if the flavour is too sharp. Pour over the salad and toss gently to coat. Sprinkle in half the mint and stir lightly.

Separate the lettuce leaves and spread onto a large shallow serving plate. Spoon the salad on top and sprinkle with the remaining mint. Garnish with mint sprigs and serve.

Try this: FOR AN ALTERNATIVE: 98 FOR ENTERTAINING: 380

Turkey & Vegetable Stir Fry

SERVES 4

350 g/12 oz mixed vegetables, such as baby sweetcorn, 1 small red pepper, pak choi, mushrooms, broccoli florets and baby carrots
1 red chilli
2 tbsp groundnut oil
350 g/12 oz skinless, boneless turkey breast, sliced into fine strips across the grain

2 garlic cloves, peeled and finely chopped
2.5 cm/1 inch piece fresh root ginger, peeled and finely grated
3 spring onions, trimmed and finely sliced
2 tbsp light soy sauce
1 tbsp Chinese rice wine or dry sherry
2 tbsp chicken stock or water
1 tsp cornflour

1 tsp sesame oil
freshly cooked noodles or rice, to serve

To garnish:
50 g/2 oz toasted cashew nuts
2 spring onions, finely shredded
25 g/1 oz beansprouts

Slice or chop the vegetables into small pieces, depending on which you use. Halve the baby sweetcorn lengthways, deseed and thinly slice the red pepper, tear or shred the pak choi, slice the mushrooms, break the broccoli into small florets and cut the carrots into matchsticks. Deseed and finely chop the chilli.

Heat a wok or large frying pan, add the oil and when hot, add the turkey strips and stir-fry for 1 minute or until they turn white. Add the garlic, ginger, spring onions and chilli and cook for a few seconds. Add the prepared carrot, pepper, broccoli and mushrooms and stir-fry for 1 minute. Add the baby sweetcorn and pak choi and stir-fry for 1 minute.

Blend the soy sauce, Chinese rice wine or sherry and stock or water and pour over the vegetables. Blend the cornflour with 1 teaspoon of water and stir into the vegetables, mixing well. Bring to the boil, reduce the heat, then simmer for 1 minute. Stir in the sesame oil. Tip into a warmed serving dish, sprinkle with cashew nuts, shredded spring onions and beansprouts. Serve immediately with noodles or rice.

Try this: FOR AN ALTERNATIVE: 96   FOR ENTERTAINING: 84

Turkey Hash with Potato & Beetroot

SERVES 4-6

2 tbsp vegetable oil
50 g/2 oz butter
4 slices streaky bacon, diced or sliced
1 medium onion, peeled and finely chopped

450 g/1 lb cooked turkey, diced
450 g/1 lb finely chopped cooked potatoes
2–3 tbsp freshly chopped parsley

2 tbsp plain flour
250 g/9 oz cooked medium beetroot, diced
green salad, to serve

In a large, heavy-based frying pan, heat the oil and half the butter over a medium heat until sizzling. Add the bacon and cook for 4 minutes, or until crisp and golden, stirring occasionally. Using a slotted spoon, transfer to a large bowl. Add the onion to the pan and cook for 3–4 minutes, or until soft and golden, stirring frequently.

Meanwhile, add the turkey, potatoes, parsley and flour to the cooked bacon in the bowl. Stir and toss gently, then fold in the diced beetroot.

Add half the remaining butter to the frying pan and then the turkey vegetable mixture. Stir, then spread the mixture to evenly cover the bottom of the frying pan. Cook for 15 minutes, or until the underside is crisp and brown, pressing the hash firmly into a cake with a spatula. Remove from the heat.

Invert a large plate over the frying pan and, holding the plate and frying pan together with an oven glove, turn the hash out onto the plate. Heat the remaining butter in the pan, slide the hash back into the pan and cook for 4 minutes, or until crisp and brown on the other side. Invert onto the plate again and serve immediately with a green salad.

Try this: FOR AN ALTERNATIVE: 82   FOR ENTERTAINING: 252

Teriyaki Turkey with Oriental Vegetables

SERVES 4

1 red chilli
1 garlic clove, peeled
   and crushed
2.5 cm/1 inch piece root
   ginger, peeled and grated
3 tbsp dark soy sauce
1 tsp sunflower oil
350 g/12 oz skinless,
   boneless turkey breast

1 tbsp sesame oil
1 tbsp sesame seeds
2 carrots, peeled and cut
   into matchstick strips
1 leek, trimmed and
   shredded
125 g/4 oz broccoli, cut
   into tiny florets
1 tsp cornflour

3 tbsp dry sherry
125 g/4 oz mangetout, cut
   into thin strips

To serve:
freshly cooked egg noodles
sprinkling of sesame seeds

Halve, deseed and thinly slice the chilli. Put into a small bowl with the garlic, ginger, soy sauce and sunflower oil. Cut the turkey into thin strips. Add to the mixture and mix until well coated. Cover with clingfilm and marinate in the refrigerator for at least 30 minutes.

Heat a wok or large frying pan. Add 2 teaspoons of the sesame oil. When hot, remove the turkey from the marinade. Stir-fry for 2–3 minutes until browned and cooked. Remove from the pan and reserve. Heat the remaining 1 teaspoon of oil in the wok. Add the sesame seeds and stir-fry for a few seconds until they start to change colour. Add the carrots, leek and broccoli and continue stir-frying for 2–3 minutes.

Blend the cornflour with 1 tablespoon of cold water to make a smooth paste. Stir in the sherry and marinade. Add to the wok with the mangetout and cook for 1 minute, stirring all the time until thickened.

Return the turkey to the pan and continue cooking for 1–2 minutes or until the turkey is hot, the vegetables are tender and the sauce is bubbling. Serve the turkey and vegetables immediately with the egg noodles. Sprinkle with the sesame seeds.

Try this: FOR AN ALTERNATIVE: 76 FOR ENTERTAINING: 70

Turkey & Mixed Mushroom Lasagne

SERVES 4

1 tbsp olive oil
225 g/8 oz mixed
    mushrooms e.g. button,
    chestnut and portabello,
    wiped and sliced
15 g/½ oz butter
25 g/1 oz plain flour
300 ml/½ pint skimmed milk
1 bay leaf

225 g/8 oz cooked
    turkey, cubed
¼ tsp freshly grated nutmeg
salt and freshly ground
    black pepper
400 g can plum tomatoes,
    drained and chopped
1 tsp dried mixed herbs
9 lasagne sheets

(about 150 g/5 oz)

For the topping:
200 ml/7 fl oz Greek yogurt
1 medium egg,
    lightly beaten
1 tbsp finely grated
    Parmesan cheese
mixed salad leaves, to serve

Preheat the oven to 180°C/350°F/Gas 4. Heat the oil and cook the mushrooms until tender and all the juices have evaporated. Remove and reserve.

Put the butter, flour, milk and bay leaf in the pan. Slowly bring to the boil, stirring until thickened. Simmer for 2–3 minutes. Remove the bay leaf and stir in the mushrooms, turkey, nutmeg, salt and pepper.

Mix together the tomatoes, mixed herbs and season with salt and pepper. Spoon half into the base of a 1.7 litre/3 pint ovenproof dish. Top with three sheets of lasagne, then with half the turkey mixture. Repeat the layers, then arrange the remaining three sheets of pasta on top.

Mix together the yogurt and egg. Spoon over the lasagne, spreading the mixture into the corners. Sprinkle with the Parmesan and bake in the preheated oven for 45 minutes. Serve with the mixed salad.

Try this: FOR AN ALTERNATIVE: 322   FOR ENTERTAINING: 338

Turkey & Oven–roasted Vegetable Salad

SERVES 4

6 tbsp olive oil

3 medium courgettes, trimmed and sliced

2 yellow peppers, deseeded and sliced

125 g/4 oz pine nuts

275 g/10 oz macaroni

350 g/12 oz cooked turkey

280 g jar or can chargrilled artichokes, drained and sliced

225 g/8 oz baby plum tomatoes, quartered

4 tbsp freshly chopped

coriander

1 garlic clove, peeled and chopped

3 tbsp balsamic vinegar

salt and freshly ground black pepper

Preheat the oven to 200°C/400°F/Gas Mark 6, 15 minutes before cooking. Line a large roasting tin with tinfoil, pour in half the olive oil and place in the oven for 3 minutes, or until very hot. Remove from the oven, add the courgettes and peppers and stir until evenly coated. Bake for 30–35 minutes, or until slightly charred, turning occasionally.

Add the pine nuts to the tin. Return to the oven and bake for 10 minutes, or until the pine nuts are toasted. Remove from the oven and allow the vegetables to cool completely.

Bring a large pan of lightly salted water to a rolling boil. Add the macaroni and cook according to the packet instructions, or until 'al dente'. Drain and refresh under cold running water then drain thoroughly and place in a large salad bowl.

Cut the turkey into bite-sized pieces and add to the macaroni. Add the artichokes and tomatoes with the cooled vegetables and pan juices to the pan. Blend together the coriander, garlic, remaining oil, vinegar and seasoning. Pour over the salad, toss lightly and serve.

 Try this: FOR AN ALTERNATIVE: 86   FOR ENTERTAINING: 52

Baked Aubergines
with Tomato & Mozzarella

SERVES 4

3 medium aubergines,
   trimmed and sliced
salt and freshly ground
   black pepper
4–6 tbsp olive oil
450 g/1 lb fresh turkey mince
1 onion, peeled and

chopped
2 garlic cloves, peeled
   and chopped
2 x 400 g cans cherry
   tomatoes
1 tbsp fresh mixed herbs
200 ml/7 fl oz red wine

350 g/12 oz macaroni
5 tbsp freshly chopped basil
125 g/4 oz mozzarella
   cheese, drained a
   nd chopped
50 g/2 oz freshly grated
   Parmesan cheese

Preheat the oven to 200˚ C/400˚F/Gas Mark 6, 15 minutes before cooking. Place the aubergine slices in a colander and sprinkle with salt. Leave for 1 hour or until the juices run clear. Rinse and dry on absorbent kitchen paper. Heat 3–5 tablespoons of the olive oil in a large frying pan and cook the prepared aubergines in batches for 2 minutes on each side, or until softened. Remove and drain on absorbent kitchen paper.

Heat 1 tablespoon of olive oil in a saucepan, add the turkey mince and cook for 5 minutes, or until browned and sealed. Add the onion to the pan and cook for 5 minutes, or until softened. Add the chopped garlic, the tomatoes and mixed herbs. Pour in the wine and season to taste with salt and pepper. Bring to the boil, lower the heat then simmer for 15 minutes, or until thickened.

Meanwhile, bring a large pan of lightly salted water to a rolling boil. Add the macaroni and cook according to the packet instructions, or until 'al dente'. Drain thoroughly.

Spoon half the tomato mixture into a lightly oiled ovenproof dish. Top with half the aubergine, pasta and chopped basil, then season lightly. Repeat the layers, finishing with a layer of aubergine. Sprinkle with the mozzarella and Parmesan cheeses, then bake in the preheated oven for 30 minutes, or until golden and bubbling. Serve immediately.

Try this: FOR AN ALTERNATIVE: 232   FOR ENTERTAINING: 222

Brown Rice & Lentil Salad with Duck

SERVES 6

225 g/8 oz Puy lentils, rinsed
4 tbsp olive oil
1 medium onion, peeled and finely chopped
200 g/7 oz long-grain brown rice
½ tsp dried thyme
450 ml/¾ pint chicken stock
salt and freshly ground black pepper
350 g/12 oz shiitake or portabella mushrooms, trimmed and sliced

375 g/13 oz cooked Chinese-style spicy duck or roasted duck, sliced into chunks
2 garlic cloves, peeled and finely chopped
125 g/4 oz cooked smoked ham, diced
2 small courgettes, trimmed, diced and blanched
6 spring onions, trimmed and thinly sliced
2 tbsp freshly

chopped parsley
2 tbsp walnut halves, toasted and chopped

For the dressing:
2 tbsp red or white wine vinegar
1 tbsp balsamic vinegar
1 tsp Dijon mustard
1 tsp clear honey
75 ml/3 fl oz extra virgin olive oil
2–3 tbsp walnut oil

Bring a large saucepan of water to the boil, sprinkle in the lentils, return to the boil, then simmer over a low heat for 30 minutes, or until tender; do not overcook. Drain and rinse under cold running water, then drain again and reserve. Heat 2 tablespoons of the oil in a saucepan. Add the onion and cook for 2 minutes until it begins to soften. Stir in the rice with the thyme and stock. Season to taste with salt and pepper and bring to the boil. Cover and simmer for 40 minutes, or until tender and the liquid is absorbed.

Heat the remaining oil in a large frying pan and add the mushrooms. Cook for 5 minutes until golden. Stir in the duck and garlic and cook for 2–3 minutes to heat through. Season well.

To make the dressing, whisk the vinegars, mustard and honey in a large serving bowl, then gradually whisk in the oils. Add the lentils and the rice, then stir lightly together. Gently stir in the ham, blanched courgettes, spring onions and parsley. Season to taste and sprinkle with the walnuts. Serve topped with the duck and mushrooms.

Try this: FOR AN ALTERNATIVE: 274   FOR ENTERTAINING: 332

Hot Duck Pasta Salad

SERVES 6

3 boneless and skinless
    duck breasts
1 tbsp wholegrain mustard
1 tbsp clear honey
salt and freshly ground
    black pepper
4 medium eggs

450 g/1 lb fusilli
125 g/4 oz French
    beans, trimmed
1 large carrot, peeled and
    cut into thin batons
125 g/4 oz sweetcorn
    kernels, cooked if frozen

75 g/3 oz fresh baby spinach
    leaves, shredded

For the dressing:
8 tbsp French dressing
1 tsp horseradish sauce
4 tbsp crème fraîche

Preheat the oven to 200°C/400°F/Gas Mark 6. Place the duck breasts on a baking tray lined with tinfoil. Mix together the wholegrain mustard and honey, season lightly with salt and pepper then spread over the duck breasts. Roast in the preheated oven for 20–30 minutes, or until tender. Remove from the oven and keep warm.

Meanwhile, place the eggs in a small saucepan, cover with water and bring to the boil. Simmer for 8 minutes, then drain. Bring a large pan of lightly salted water to a rolling boil. Add the beans and pasta, return to the boil and cook according to the packet instructions, or until 'al dente'. Drain the pasta and beans and refresh under cold running water.

Place the pasta and beans in a bowl, add the carrot, sweetcorn and spinach leaves and toss lightly. Shell the eggs, cut into wedges and arrange on top of the pasta. Slice the duck breasts then place them on top of the salad. Beat the dressing ingredients together in a bowl until well blended, then drizzle over the salad. Serve immediately.

Try this: FOR AN ALTERNATIVE: 110   FOR ENTERTAINING: 116

Teriyaki Duck with Plum Chutney

SERVES 4

4 tbsp Japanese soy sauce
4 tbsp dry sherry
2 garlic cloves, peeled and
  finely chopped
2.5 cm/1 inch piece fresh
  root ginger, peeled and
  finely chopped
350 g/12 oz skinless
  duck breast fillets,
cut in chunks
2 tbsp groundnut oil
225 g/8 oz carrots, peeled
  and cut into fine strips
½ cucumber, cut into strips
5 spring onions, trimmed
  and shredded
toasted almonds, to garnish
freshly cooked egg
noodles, to serve
For the plum chutney:
25 g/1 oz butter
1 red onion, peeled and
  finely chopped
2 tsp soft brown sugar
4 plums, stoned and halved
zest and juice of ½ orange
50 g/2 oz raisins

Mix together the soy sauce, sherry, garlic and ginger and pour into a shallow dish. Add the duck strips and stir until coated in the marinade. Cover and leave in the refrigerator for 30 minutes.

Meanwhile make the plum chutney. Melt the butter in a wok, add the onion and sugar and cook gently over a low heat for 20 minutes. Add the plums, orange zest and juice and simmer for 10 minutes, then stir in the raisins. Spoon into a small bowl and wipe the wok clean. Drain the duck, reserving the marinade.

Heat the wok, add the oil and when hot, add the carrots, cucumber and spring onions. Stir-fry for 2 minutes, or until tender. Remove and reserve. Add the drained duck to the wok and stir-fry over a high heat for 2 minutes. Return the vegetables to the wok and add the reserved marinade. Stir-fry briefly, until heated through.

Garnish the duck with the toasted almonds and serve immediately with freshly cooked noodles and the plum chutney.

Try this: FOR AN ALTERNATIVE: 126   FOR ENTERTAINING: 140

Stir-fried Duck with Cashews

SERVES 4

450 g/1 lb duck breast,
skinned
3 tbsp groundnut oil
1 garlic clove, peeled and
finely chopped
1 tsp freshly grated
ginger root

1 carrot, peeled and sliced
125 g/4 oz mangetout,
trimmed
2 tsp Chinese rice wine
or dry sherry
1 tbsp light soy sauce
1 tsp cornflour

50 g/2 oz unsalted cashew
nuts, roasted
1 spring onion, trimmed and
finely chopped
1 spring onion, shredded
boiled or steamed rice,
to serve

Trim the duck breasts, discarding any fat and slice thickly. Heat the wok, add 2 tablespoons of the oil and when hot, add the sliced duck breast. Cook for 3–4 minutes or until sealed. Using a slotted spoon, remove from the wok and leave to drain on absorbent kitchen paper.

Wipe the wok clean and return to the heat. Add the remaining oil and when hot, add the garlic and ginger. Stir-fry for 30 seconds, then add the carrot and mangetout. Stir-fry for a further 2 minutes, then pour in the Chinese rice wine or sherry and soy sauce.

Blend the cornflour with 1 teaspoon of water and stir into the wok. Mix well and bring to the boil. Return the duck slices to the wok and simmer for 5 minutes, or until the meat and vegetables are tender. Add the cashews, then remove the wok from the heat.

Sprinkle over the chopped and shredded spring onion and serve immediately with plain boiled or steamed rice.

Try this: FOR AN ALTERNATIVE: 138   FOR ENTERTAINING: 136

Vegetarian

Stilton, Tomato & Courgette Quiche

SERVES 4

1 quantity shop-bought
  shortcrust pastry
25 g/1 oz butter
1 onion, peeled and
  finely chopped

1 courgette, trimmed
  and sliced
125 g/4 oz Stilton
  cheese, crumbled
6 cherry tomatoes, halved

2 large eggs, beaten
200 ml tub crème fraîche
salt and freshly ground
  black pepper

Preheat the oven to 190°C/375°F/Gas Mark 5. On a lightly floured surface, roll out the pastry and use to line an 18 cm/7 inch lightly oiled quiche or flan tin, trimming any excess pastry with a knife.

Prick the base all over with a fork and bake blind in the preheated oven for 15 minutes. Remove the pastry from the oven and brush with a little of the beaten egg. Return to the oven for a further 5 minutes.

Heat the butter in a frying pan and gently fry the onion and courgette for about 4 minutes until soft and starting to brown. Transfer into the pastry case.

Sprinkle the Stilton over evenly and top with the halved cherry tomatoes. Beat together the eggs and crème fraîche and season to taste with salt and pepper.

Pour the filling into the pastry case and bake in the oven for 35–40 minutes, or until the filling is golden brown and set in the centre. Serve the quiche hot or cold.

Try this: FOR AN ALTERNATIVE: 148   FOR ENTERTAINING: 162

French Onion Tart

SERVES 4

For the quick
   flaky pastry:
125 g/4 oz butter
175 g/6 oz plain flour
pinch of salt

For the filling:
2 tbsp olive oil
4 large onions, peeled and
   thinly sliced
3 tbsp white wine vinegar
2 tbsp muscovado sugar

a little beaten egg or milk
175 g/6 oz Cheddar
   cheese, grated
salt and freshly ground
   black pepper

Preheat the oven to 200°C/400°F/Gas Mark 6. Place the butter in the freezer for 30 minutes. Sift the flour and salt into a large bowl. Remove the butter from the freezer and grate using the coarse side of a grater, dipping the butter in the flour every now and again, as it makes it easier to grate. Mix the butter into the flour, using a knife, making sure all the butter is coated thoroughly with flour. Add 2 tablespoons of cold water and continue to mix, bringing the mixture together. Use your hands to complete the mixing. Add a little more water if needed to leave a clean bowl. Place the pastry in a polythene bag and chill in the refrigerator for 30 minutes.

Heat the oil in a large frying pan, then fry the onions for 10 minutes, stirring occasionally until softened. Stir in the white wine vinegar and sugar. Increase the heat and stir frequently, for another 4–5 minutes, until the onions turn a deep caramel colour. Cook for another 5 minutes, then reserve to cool.

On a lightly floured surface, roll out the pastry to a 35.5 cm/14 inch circle. Wrap over a rolling pin and move the circle on to a baking sheet. Sprinkle half the cheese over the pastry, leaving a 5 cm/2 inch border around the edge, then spoon the caramelised onions over the cheese. Fold the uncovered pastry edges over the edge of the filling to form a rim and brush the rim with beaten egg or milk. Season to taste with salt and pepper. Sprinkle over the remaining Cheddar and bake for 20–25 minutes. Transfer to a large plate and serve immediately.

Try this: FOR AN ALTERNATIVE: 154   FOR ENTERTAINING: 152

Parsnip Tatin

SERVES 4

1 quantity shop-bought
   shortcrust pastry

For the filling:
50 g/2 oz butter
8 small parsnips, peeled

   and halved
1 tbsp brown sugar
75 ml/3 fl oz apple juice

Preheat the oven to 200°C/400°F/Gas Mark 6. Heat the butter in a 20.5 cm/8 inch frying pan. Add the parsnips, arranging the cut side down with the narrow ends towards the centre.

Sprinkle the parsnips with sugar and cook for 15 minutes, turning halfway through until golden. Add the apple juice and bring to the boil. Remove the pan from the heat.

On a lightly floured surface, roll the pastry out to a size slightly larger than the frying pan. Position the pastry over the parsnips and press down slightly to enclose the parsnips.

Bake in the preheated oven for 20–25 minutes until the parsnips and pastry are golden.

Invert a warm serving plate over the pan and carefully turn the pan over to flip the tart on to the plate. Serve immediately.

Try this: FOR AN ALTERNATIVE: 144   FOR ENTERTAINING: 166

Fennel & Caramelised Shallot Tartlets

SERVES 6

For the cheese pastry:
176 g/6 oz plain white flour
75 g/3 oz slightly
  salted butter
50 g/2 oz Gruyère
  cheese, grated
1 small egg yolk

For the filling:
2 tbsp olive oil
225 g/8 oz shallots,
  peeled and halved
1 fennel bulb, trimmed
  and sliced
1 tsp soft brown sugar
1 medium egg

150 ml/¼ pint double cream
salt and freshly ground
  black pepper
25 g/1 oz Gruyère
  cheese, grated
½ tsp ground cinnamon
mixed salad leaves, to serve

Preheat the oven to 200°C/400°F/Gas Mark 6. Sift the flour into a bowl, then rub in the butter, using your fingertips. Stir in the cheese, then add the egg yolk with about 2 tablespoons of cold water. Mix to a firm dough, then knead lightly. Wrap in clingfilm and chill in the refrigerator for 30 minutes.

Roll out the pastry on a lightly floured surface and use to line six 10 cm/4 inch individual flan tins or patty tins which are about 2 cm/¾ inch deep. Line the pastry cases with greaseproof paper and fill with baking beans or rice. Bake blind in the preheated oven for about 10 minutes, then remove the paper and beans.

Heat the oil in a frying pan, add the shallots and fennel and fry gently for 5 minutes. Sprinkle with the sugar and cook for a further 10 minutes, stirring occasionally until lightly caramelised. Reserve until cooled.

Beat together the egg and cream and season to taste with salt and pepper. Divide the shallot mixture between the pastry cases. Pour over the egg mixture and sprinkle with the cheese and cinnamon. Bake for 20 minutes, until golden and set. Serve with the salad leaves.

Try this: FOR AN ALTERNATIVE: 148 FOR ENTERTAINING: 146

Red Pepper & Basil Tart

SERVES 4-6

For the olive pastry:
225 g/8 oz plain flour
pinch of salt
50 g/2 oz pitted black olives,
    finely chopped
1 medium egg, lightly
    beaten, plus 1 egg yolk

3 tbsp olive oil
For the filling:
2 large red peppers,
    quartered and deseeded
175 g/6 oz mascarpone
    cheese
4 tbsp milk

2 medium eggs
3 tbsp freshly chopped basil
salt and freshly ground
    black pepper
sprig of fresh basil,
    to garnish
mixed salad, to serve

Preheat the oven to 200°C/400°F/Gas Mark 6, 15 minutes before cooking. Sift the flour and salt into a bowl. Make a well in the centre. Stir together the egg, oil and 1 tablespoon of tepid water. Add to the dry ingredients, drop in the olives and mix to a dough. Knead on a lightly floured surface for a few seconds until smooth, then wrap in clingfilm and chill in the refrigerator for 30 minutes. Roll out the pastry and use to line a 23 cm/9 inch loose-bottomed fluted flan tin. Lightly prick the base with a fork. Cover and chill in the refrigerator for 20 minutes.

Cook the peppers under a hot grill for 10 minutes, or until the skins are blackened and blistered. Put the peppers in a plastic bag, cool for 10 minutes, then remove the skin and slice. Line the pastry case with tinfoil or greaseproof paper weighed down with baking beans and bake in the preheated oven for 10 minutes. Remove the tinfoil and beans and bake for a further 5 minutes. Reduce the oven temperature to 180°C/350°F/Gas Mark 4.

Beat the mascarpone cheese until smooth. Gradually add the milk and eggs. Stir in the peppers, basil and season to taste with salt and pepper. Spoon into the flan case and bake for 25–30 minutes, or until lightly set. Garnish with a sprig of fresh basil and serve immediately with a mixed salad.

Try this: FOR AN ALTERNATIVE: 162   FOR ENTERTAINING: 158

Roasted Vegetable Pie

SERVES 4

225 g/8 oz plain flour
pinch of salt
50 g/2 oz white vegetable fat
   or lard, cut into squares
50 g/2 oz butter, cut
   into squares
2 tsp herbes de Provence
1 red pepper, deseeded
   and halved

1 green pepper, deseeded
   and halved
1 yellow pepper, deseeded
   and halved
3 tbsp extra virgin olive oil
1 aubergine, trimmed
   and sliced
1 courgette, trimmed and
   halved lengthways

1 leek, trimmed and cut
   into chunks
1 medium egg, beaten
125 g/4 oz fresh mozzarella
   cheese, sliced
salt and freshly ground
   black pepper
sprigs of mixed herbs,
   to garnish

Preheat the oven to 220°C/425°F/Gas Mark 7. Sift the flour and salt into a large bowl, add the fats and mix lightly until the mixture resembles breadcrumbs. Stir in the herbs. Sprinkle over a tablespoon of cold water and with a knife start bringing the dough together – it may be necessary to use your hands for the final stage. Add a little more water if needed. Place the pastry in a polythene bag and chill for 30 minutes. Place the peppers on a baking tray and sprinkle with 1 tablespoon of oil. Roast in the preheated oven for 20 minutes or until the skins start to blacken. Brush the aubergines, courgettes and leeks with oil and place on another baking tray. Roast in the oven with the peppers for 20 minutes. Place the blackened peppers in a polythene bag and leave the skin to loosen for 5 minutes. When cool enough to handle, peel the skins off the peppers.

Roll out half the pastry on a lightly floured surface and use to line a 20.5 cm/8 inch round pie dish. Line the pastry with greaseproof paper and fill with baking beans and bake blind for about 10 minutes. Remove the beans and the paper, then brush the base with a little of the beaten egg. Return to the oven for 5 minutes. Layer the cooked vegetables and the cheese in the pastry case, seasoning each layer. Roll out the remaining pastry on a lightly floured surface, and cut out the lid 5 mm/¼ inch wider than the dish. Brush the rim with the beaten egg and lay the pastry lid on top, pressing to seal. Cut a slit in the lid and brush with the beaten egg. Bake for 30 minutes. Transfer to a large serving dish, garnish with sprigs of mixed herbs and serve.

Try this: FOR AN ALTERNATIVE: 146   FOR ENTERTAINING: 152

Spinach, Pine Nut & Mascarpone Pizza

SERVES 2-4

For the basic pizza dough:
225 g/8 oz strong plain flour
½ tsp salt
¼ tsp quick-acting
    dried yeast
150 ml/¼ pint warm water
1 tbsp extra virgin olive oil

For the topping:
3 tbsp olive oil
1 large red onion, peeled
    and chopped
2 garlic cloves, peeled and
    finely sliced
450 g/1 lb frozen spinach,

thawed and drained
salt and freshly ground
    black pepper
3 tbsp passata
125 g/4 oz mascarpone
    cheese
1 tbsp toasted pine nuts

Preheat the oven to 220°C/425°F/Gas Mark 7. Sift the flour and salt into a bowl and stir in the yeast. Make a well in the centre and gradually add the water and oil to form soft dough. Knead the dough on a floured surface for about 5 minutes until smooth and elastic. Place in a lightly oiled bowl and cover with clingfilm. Leave to rise in a warm place for 1 hour.

Knock the pizza dough with your fist a few times, shape and roll out thinly on a lightly floured board. Place on a lightly floured baking sheet and lift the edge to make a little rim. Place another baking sheet into the preheated oven to heat up.

Heat half the oil in a frying pan and gently fry the onion and garlic until soft and starting to change colour. Squeeze out any excess water from the spinach and finely chop. Add to the onion and garlic with the remaining olive oil. Season to taste with salt and pepper.

Spread the passata on the pizza dough and top with the spinach mixture. Mix the mascarpone with the pine nuts and dot over the pizza.

Slide the pizza on to the hot baking sheet and bake for 15–20 minutes. Transfer to a large plate and serve immediately.

Try this: FOR AN ALTERNATIVE: 158   FOR ENTERTAINING: 160

Three Tomato Pizza

SERVES 2-4

1 quantity pizza dough (see page 156)	6 sun-dried tomatoes	125 g/4 oz buffalo mozzarella cheese, sliced
3 plum tomatoes	pinch of sea salt	freshly ground black pepper
8 cherry tomatoes	1 tbsp freshly chopped basil	fresh basil leaves, to garnish
	2 tbsp extra virgin olive oil	

Preheat the oven to 220°C/425°F/Gas Mark 7. Place a baking sheet into the oven to heat up.

Divide the prepared pizza dough into four equal pieces. Roll out one quarter of the pizza dough on a lightly floured board to form a 20.5 cm/8 inch round.

Roll out the other three pieces into rounds, one at a time. While rolling out any piece of dough, keep the others covered with clingfilm.

Slice the plum tomatoes, halve the cherry tomatoes and chop the sun-dried tomatoes into small pieces. Place a few pieces of each type of tomato on each pizza base then season to taste with the sea salt.

Sprinkle with the chopped basil and drizzle with the olive oil. Place a few slices of mozzarella on each pizza and season with black pepper.

Transfer the pizza on to the heated baking sheet and cook for 15–20 minutes, or until the cheese is golden brown and bubbling. Garnish with the basil leaves and serve immediately.

Try this: FOR AN ALTERNATIVE: 160   FOR ENTERTAINING: 156

Chargrilled Vegetable & Goats' Cheese Pizza

SERVES 4

125 g/4 oz baking potato
1 tbsp olive oil
225 g/8 oz strong white flour
½ tsp salt
1 tsp easy-blend dried yeast

For the topping:
1 medium aubergine,
   thinly sliced

2 small courgettes, trimmed
   and sliced lengthways
1 yellow pepper, quartered
   and deseeded
1 red onion, peeled
   and sliced into very
   thin wedges
5 tbsp olive oil
175 g/6 oz cooked new

potatoes, halved
400 g can chopped
   tomatoes, drained
2 tsp freshly chopped
   oregano
125 g/4 oz mozzarella cheese,
   cut into small cubes
125 g/4 oz goats' cheese,
   crumbled

Preheat the oven to 220°C/425°F/Gas Mark 7, 15 minutes before baking. Put a baking sheet in the oven to heat up. Cook the potato in lightly salted boiling water until tender. Peel and mash with the olive oil until smooth. Sift the flour and salt into a bowl. Stir in the yeast. Add the mashed potato and 150 ml/¼ pint warm water and mix to a soft dough. Knead for 5–6 minutes, until smooth. Put the dough in a bowl, cover with clingfilm and leave to rise in a warm place for 30 minutes.

To make the topping, arrange the aubergine, courgettes, pepper and onion, skin-side up, on a grill rack and brush with 4 tablespoons of the oil. Grill for 4–5 minutes. Turn the vegetables and brush with the remaining oil. Grill for 3–4 minutes. Cool, skin and slice the pepper. Put all of the vegetables in a bowl, add the halved new potatoes and toss gently together. Set aside.

Briefly re-knead the dough then roll out to a 30.5–35.5 cm/12–14 inch round, according to preferred thickness. Mix the tomatoes and oregano together and spread over the pizza base. Scatter over the mozzarella cheese. Put the pizza on the preheated baking sheet and bake for 8 minutes. Arrange the vegetables and goats' cheese on top and bake for 8–10 minutes.

Try this: FOR AN ALTERNATIVE: 152   FOR ENTERTAINING: 154

Tomato & Courgette Herb Tart

SERVES 4

4 tbsp olive oil
1 onion, peeled and
   finely chopped
3 garlic cloves,
   peeled and crushed
400 g/14 oz prepared puff
   pastry, thawed if frozen

1 small egg, beaten
2 tbsp freshly chopped
   rosemary
2 tbsp freshly
   chopped parsley
175 g/6 oz rindless fresh soft
   goats' cheese

4 ripe plum
   tomatoes, sliced
1 medium courgette,
   trimmed and sliced
thyme sprigs, to garnish

Preheat the oven to 230°C/450°F/Gas Mark 8. Heat 2 tablespoons of the oil in a large frying pan. Fry the onion and garlic for about 4 minutes until softened and reserve.

Roll out the pastry on a lightly floured surface, and cut out a 30.5 cm/12 inch circle. Brush the pastry with a little beaten egg, then prick all over with a fork. Transfer on to a dampened baking sheet and bake in the preheated oven for 10 minutes.

Turn the pastry over and brush with a little more egg. Bake for 5 more minutes, then remove from the oven.

Mix together the onion, garlic and herbs with the goats' cheese and spread over the pastry. Arrange the tomatoes and courgettes over the goats' cheese and drizzle with the remaining oil.

Bake for 20–25 minutes, or until the pastry is golden brown and the topping bubbling. Garnish with the thyme sprigs and serve immediately.

Try this: FOR AN ALTERNATIVE: 144   FOR ENTERTAINING: 152

Leek & Potato Tart

SERVES 6

225 g/8 oz plain flour
pinch of salt
150 g/5 oz butter, cubed
50 g/2 oz walnuts, very
   finely chopped
1 large egg yolk

For the filling:
450 g/1 lb leeks, trimmed
   and thinly sliced
40 g/1½ oz butter
450 g/1 lb large new
   potatoes, scrubbed
300 ml/½ pint soured cream

3 medium eggs,
   lightly beaten
175 g/6 oz Gruyère
   cheese, grated
freshly grated nutmeg
salt and fresh black pepper
fresh chives, to garnish

Preheat the oven to 200°C/400°F/Gas Mark 6, about 15 minutes before baking. Sift the flour and salt into a bowl. Rub in the butter until the mixture resembles breadcrumbs. Stir in the nuts. Mix together the egg yolk and 3 tablespoons of cold water. Sprinkle over the dry ingredients. Mix to form a dough.

Knead on a lightly floured surface for a few seconds, then wrap in clingfilm and chill in the refrigerator for 20 minutes. Roll out and use to line a 20.5 cm/8 inch spring-form tin or very deep flan tin. Chill for a further 30 minutes.

Cook the leeks in the butter over a high heat for 2–3 minutes, stirring constantly. Lower the heat, cover and cook for 25 minutes until soft, stirring occasionally. Remove the leeks from the heat. Cook the potatoes in boiling salted water for 15 minutes, or until almost tender. Drain and thickly slice. Add to the leeks. Stir the soured cream into the leeks and potatoes, followed by the eggs, cheese, nutmeg and salt and pepper. Pour into the pastry case and bake on the middle shelf in the preheated oven for 20 minutes.

Reduce the oven temperature to 190°C/375°F/Gas Mark 5 and cook for a further 30–35 minutes, or until the filling is set. Garnish with chives and serve immediately.

Try this: FOR AN ALTERNATIVE: 154   FOR ENTERTAINING: 162

Courgette & Tarragon Tortilla

SERVES 6

700 g/1½ lb potatoes
3 tbsp olive oil
1 onion, peeled and
    thinly sliced

salt and freshly ground
    black pepper
1 courgette, trimmed and
    thinly sliced

6 medium eggs
2 tbsp freshly chopped
    tarragon
tomato wedges, to serve

Peel the potatoes and thinly slice. Dry the slices in a clean tea towel to get them as dry as possible. Heat the oil in a large heavy-based pan, add the onion and cook for 3 minutes. Add the potatoes with a little salt and pepper, then stir the potatoes and onion lightly to coat in the oil.

Reduce the heat to the lowest possible setting, cover and cook gently for 5 minutes. Turn the potatoes and onion over and continue to cook for a further 5 minutes. Give the pan a shake every now and again to ensure that the potatoes do not stick to the base or burn. Add the courgette, then cover and cook for a further 10 minutes.

Beat the eggs and tarragon together and season to taste with salt and pepper. Pour the egg mixture over the vegetables and return to the heat. Cook on a low heat for up to 20–25 minutes, or until there is no liquid egg left on the surface of the tortilla.

Turn the tortilla over by inverting the tortilla onto the lid or onto a flat plate. Return the pan to the heat and cook for a final 3–5 minutes, or until the underside is golden brown. If preferred, place the tortilla under a preheated grill for 4 minutes, or until set and golden brown on top. Cut into small squares and serve hot or cold with tomato wedges.

Try this: FOR AN ALTERNATIVE: 236   FOR ENTERTAINING: 82

Sweet Potato Crisps with Mango Salsa

SERVES 6

For the salsa:
1 large mango, peeled, stoned and cut into small cubes
8 cherry tomatoes, quartered
½ cucumber, peeled if preferred and finely diced
1 red onion, peeled and finely chopped
pinch of sugar
1 red chilli, deseeded and finely chopped
2 tbsp rice vinegar
2 tbsp olive oil
grated rind and juice of 1 lime
450 g/1 lb sweet potatoes, peeled and thinly sliced
vegetable oil, for deep frying
sea salt
2 tbsp freshly chopped mint

To make the salsa, mix the mango with the tomatoes, cucumber and onion. Add the sugar, chilli, vinegar, oil and the lime rind and juice. Mix together thoroughly, cover and leave for 45–50 minutes.

Soak the potatoes in cold water for 40 minutes to remove as much of the excess starch as possible. Drain and dry thoroughly in a clean tea towel, or absorbent kitchen paper.

Heat the oil to 190°C/375°F in a deep fryer. When at the correct temperature, place half the potatoes in the frying basket, then carefully lower the potatoes into the hot oil and cook for 4–5 minutes, or until they are golden brown, shaking the basket every minute so that they do not stick together.

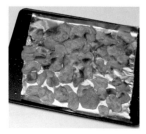

Drain the potato crisps on absorbent kitchen paper, sprinkle with sea salt and place under a preheated moderate grill for a few seconds to dry out. Repeat with the remaining potatoes. Stir the mint into the salsa and serve with the potato crisps.

Try this: FOR AN ALTERNATIVE: 344   FOR ENTERTAINING: 334

Swede, Turnip, Parsnip & Potato Soup

SERVES 4

2 large onions, peeled
25 g/1 oz butter
2 medium carrots, peeled
and roughly chopped
175 g/6 oz swede, peeled
and roughly chopped
125 g/4 oz turnip, peeled and

roughly chopped
125 g/4 oz parsnips, peeled
and roughly chopped
175 g/6 oz potatoes, peeled
1 litre/1¾ pints vegetable
stock
½ tsp freshly grated nutmeg

salt and freshly ground
black pepper
4 tbsp vegetable oil,
for frying
125 ml/4 fl oz double cream
warm crusty bread,
to serve

Finely chop 1 onion. Melt the butter in a large saucepan and add the onion, carrots, swede, turnip, parsnip and potatoes. Cover and cook gently for about 10 minutes, without colouring. Stir occasionally during this time.

Add the stock and season to taste with the nutmeg, salt and pepper. Cover and bring to the boil, then reduce the heat and simmer gently for 15–20 minutes, or until the vegetables are tender. Remove from the heat and leave to cool for 30 minutes.

Heat the oil in a large, heavy-based frying pan. Add the onions and cook over a medium heat, for about 2–3 minutes, stirring frequently, until golden brown. Remove the onions with a slotted spoon and drain well on absorbent kitchen paper. As they cool, they will turn crispy.

Pour the cooled soup into a food processor or blender and process to form a smooth purée. Return to the cleaned pan, adjust the seasoning, then stir in the cream. Gently reheat and top with the crispy onions. Serve immediately with chunks of bread.

Try this: FOR AN ALTERNATIVE: 276   FOR ENTERTAINING: 280

Spring Vegetable & Herb Risotto

SERVES 2-3

1 litre/1¾ pint
  vegetable stock
125 g/4 oz asparagus
  tips, trimmed
125 g/4 oz baby
  carrots, scrubbed
50 g/2 oz peas, fresh
  or frozen

50 g/2 oz fine French
  beans, trimmed
1 tbsp olive oil
1 onion, peeled and
  finely chopped
1 garlic clove, peeled and
  finely chopped
2 tsp freshly chopped thyme

225 g/8 oz risotto rice
150 ml/¼ pint white wine
1 tbsp each freshly chopped
  basil, chives and parsley
zest of ½ lemon
3 tbsp crème fraîche
salt and freshly ground
  black pepper

Bring the vegetable stock to the boil in a large saucepan and add the asparagus, baby carrots, peas and beans. Bring the stock back to the boil and remove the vegetables at once using a slotted spoon. Rinse under cold running water. Drain again and reserve. Keep the stock hot.

Heat the oil in a large deep frying pan and add the onion. Cook over a medium heat for 4–5 minutes until starting to brown. Add the garlic and thyme and cook for a further few seconds. Add the rice and stir well for a minute until the rice is hot and coated in oil.

Add the white wine and stir constantly until the wine is almost completely absorbed by the rice. Begin adding the stock a ladleful at a time, stirring well and waiting until the last ladleful has been absorbed before stirring in the next. Add the vegetables after using about half of the stock. Continue until all the stock is used. This will take 20–25 minutes. The rice and vegetables should both be tender.

Remove the pan from the heat. Stir in the herbs, lemon zest and crème fraîche. Season to taste with salt and pepper and serve immediately.

Try this: FOR AN ALTERNATIVE: 254   FOR ENTERTAINING: 248

Baby Onion Risotto

SERVES 4

For the baby onions:
1 tbsp olive oil
450 g/1 lb baby onions,
    peeled and halved
    if large
pinch of sugar
1 tbsp freshly chopped
    thyme

For the risotto:
1 tbsp olive oil
1 small onion, peeled
    and finely chopped
2 garlic cloves, peeled
    and finely chopped
350 g/12 oz risotto rice
150 ml/¼ pint red wine
1 litre/1¾ pint hot

vegetable stock
125 g/4 oz soft
    goats' cheese
salt and freshly ground
    black pepper
sprigs of fresh thyme,
    to garnish
rocket leaves, to serve

For the baby onions, heat the olive oil in a saucepan and add the onions with the sugar. Cover and cook over a low heat, stirring occasionally, for 20–25 minutes until caramelised. Uncover during the last 10 minutes of cooking.

Meanwhile, for the risotto, heat the oil in a large frying pan and add the onion. Cook over a medium heat for 5 minutes until softened. Add the garlic and cook for a further 30 seconds.

Add the risotto rice and stir well. Add the red wine and stir constantly until the wine is almost completely absorbed by the rice. Begin adding the stock a ladleful at a time, stirring well and waiting until the last ladleful has been absorbed before stirring in the next. It will take 20–25 minutes to add all the stock by which time the rice should be just cooked but still firm. Remove from the heat.

Add the thyme to the onions and cook briefly. Increase the heat and allow the onion mixture to bubble for 2–3 minutes until almost evaporated. Add the onion mixture to the risotto along with the goats' cheese. Stir well and season to taste with salt and pepper. Garnish with sprigs of fresh thyme. Serve immediately with the rocket leaves.

Try this: FOR AN ALTERNATIVE: 266   FOR ENTERTAINING: 242

Ginger & Garlic Potatoes

SERVES 4

700 g/1½ lb potatoes
2.5 cm/1 inch piece of root
  ginger, peeled and
  coarsely chopped
3 garlic cloves, peeled
  and chopped
½ tsp turmeric

1 tsp salt
½ tsp cayenne pepper
5 tbsp vegetable oil
1 tsp whole fennel seeds
1 large eating apple, cored
  and diced
6 spring onions, trimmed

and sliced diagonally
1 tbsp freshly chopped
  coriander

To serve:
assorted bitter salad leaves
curry-flavoured mayonnaise

Scrub the potatoes, then place, unpeeled, in a large saucepan and cover with boiling salted water. Bring to the boil and cook for 15 minutes, then drain and leave the potatoes to cool completely. Peel and cut into 2.5 cm/1 inch cubes.

Place the root ginger, garlic, turmeric, salt and cayenne pepper in a food processor and blend for 1 minute. With the motor still running, slowly add 3 tablespoons of water and blend into a paste. Alternatively, pound the ingredients to a paste with a pestle and mortar.

Heat the oil in a large, heavy-based frying pan and when hot, but not smoking, add the fennel seeds and fry for a few minutes. Stir in the ginger paste and cook for 2 minutes, stirring frequently. Take care not to burn the mixture.

Reduce the heat, then add the potatoes and cook for 5–7 minutes, stirring frequently, until the potatoes have a golden-brown crust. Add the diced apple and spring onions, then sprinkle with the freshly chopped coriander. Heat through for 2 minutes, then serve on assorted salad leaves with curry-flavoured mayonnaise.

Try this: FOR AN ALTERNATIVE: 218   FOR ENTERTAINING: 252

Winter Coleslaw

SERVES 6

175 g/6 oz white cabbage
1 medium red onion, peeled
175 g/6 oz carrot, peeled
175 g/6 oz celeriac, peeled
2 celery stalks, trimmed

75 g/3 oz golden sultanas
For the yogurt &
  herb dressing:
150 ml/¼ pint natural yogurt
1 garlic clove, peeled

  and crushed
1 tbsp lemon juice
1 tsp clear honey
1 tbsp freshly snipped
  chives

Remove the hard core from the cabbage with a small knife and shred finely. Slice the onion finely and coarsely grate the carrot. Place the raw vegetables in a large bowl and mix together.

Cut the celeriac into thin strips and simmer in boiling water for about 2 minutes. Drain the celeriac and rinse thoroughly with cold water.

Chop the celery and add to the bowl with the celeriac and sultanas and mix well.

Make the yogurt and herb dressing by briskly whisking the yogurt, garlic, lemon juice, honey and chives together.

Pour the dressing over the top of the salad. Stir the vegetables thoroughly to coat evenly and serve.

Try this: FOR AN ALTERNATIVE: 246 FOR ENTERTAINING: 366

Carrot, Celeriac & Sesame Seed Salad

SERVES 6

225 g/8 oz celeriac
225 g/8 oz carrots, peeled
50 g/2 oz seedless raisins
2 tbsp sesame seeds
freshly chopped parsley,
    to garnish

For the lemon &
    chilli dressing:
grated rind of 1 lemon
4 tbsp lemon juice
2 tbsp sunflower oil
2 tbsp clear honey

1 red bird's eye
    chilli, deseeded and
    finely chopped
salt and freshly ground
    black pepper

Slice the celeriac into thin matchsticks. Place in a small saucepan of boiling salted water and boil for 2 minutes.

Drain and rinse the celeriac in cold water and place in a mixing bowl. Finely grate the carrot. Add the carrot and the raisins to the celeriac in the bowl.

Place the sesame seeds under a hot grill or dry-fry in a frying pan for 1–2 minutes until golden brown, then leave to cool.

Make the dressing by whisking together the lemon rind, lemon juice, oil, honey, chilli and seasoning or by shaking thoroughly in a screw-topped jar.

Pour 2 tablespoons of the dressing over the salad and toss well. Turn into a serving dish and sprinkle over the toasted sesame seeds and chopped parsley. Serve the remaining dressing separately.

Try this: FOR AN ALTERNATIVE: 340   FOR ENTERTAINING: 110

Spiced Couscous & Vegetables

SERVES 4

1 tbsp olive oil
1 large shallot, peeled
and finely chopped
1 garlic clove, peeled
and finely chopped
1 small red pepper,
deseeded and cut
into strips
1 small yellow pepper,
deseeded and cut
into strips

1 small aubergine, diced
1 tsp each turmeric, ground
cumin, ground cinnamon
and paprika
2 tsp ground coriander
large pinch saffron strands
2 tomatoes, peeled,
deseeded and diced
2 tbsp lemon juice
225 g/8 oz couscous
225 ml/8 fl oz vegetable

stock
2 tbsp raisins
2 tbsp whole almonds
2 tbsp freshly chopped
parsley
2 tbsp freshly
chopped coriander
salt and freshly ground
black pepper

Heat the oil in a large frying pan and add the shallot and garlic and cook for 2–3 minutes until softened. Add the peppers and aubergine and reduce the heat. Cook for 8–10 minutes until the vegetables are tender, adding a little water if necessary. Test a piece of aubergine to ensure it is cooked through. Add all the spices and cook for a further minute, stirring.

Increase the heat and add the tomatoes and lemon juice. Cook for 2–3 minutes until the tomatoes have started to break down. Remove from the heat and leave to cool slightly.

Meanwhile, put the couscous into a large bowl. Bring the stock to the boil in a saucepan, then pour over the couscous. Stir well and cover with a clean tea towel. Leave to stand for 7–8 minutes until all the stock is absorbed and the couscous is tender.

Uncover the couscous and fluff with a fork. Stir in the vegetable and spice mixture along with the raisins, almonds, parsley and coriander. Season to taste with salt and pepper and serve.

Try this: FOR AN ALTERNATIVE: 304   FOR ENTERTAINING: 196

Black Bean Chilli with Avocado Salsa

SERVES 4

250 g/9 oz black beans
  and black-eye beans,
  soaked overnight
2 tbsp olive oil
1 large onion, peeled
  and finely chopped
1 red pepper, deseeded
  and diced
2 garlic cloves, peeled
  and finely chopped
1 red chilli, deseeded
  and finely chopped

2 tsp chilli powder
1 tsp ground cumin
2 tsp ground coriander
400 g can chopped tomatoes
450 ml/¾ pint vegetable
  stock
1 small ripe avocado, diced
½ small red onion, peeled
  and finely chopped
2 tbsp freshly
  chopped coriander
juice of 1 lime

1 small tomato, peeled,
  deseeded and diced
salt and freshly ground
  black pepper
25 g/1 oz dark chocolate

To garnish:
crème fraîche
lime slices
sprigs of coriander

Drain the beans and place in a large saucepan with at least twice their volume of fresh water. Bring slowly to the boil, skimming off any froth that rises to the surface. Boil rapidly for 10 minutes, then reduce the heat and simmer for about 45 minutes, adding more water if necessary. Drain and reserve.

Heat the oil in a large saucepan and add the onion and pepper. Cook for 3–4 minutes until softened. Add the garlic and chilli. Cook for 5 minutes, or until the onion and pepper have softened. Add the chilli powder, cumin and coriander and cook for 30 seconds. Add the beans along with the tomatoes and stock. Bring to the boil and simmer uncovered for 40–45 minutes until the beans and vegetables are tender and the sauce has reduced.

Mix together the avocado, onion, fresh coriander, lime juice and tomato. Season with salt and pepper and set aside. Remove the chilli from the heat. Break the chocolate into pieces. Sprinkle over the chilli. Leave for 2 minutes. Stir well. Garnish with crème fraîche, lime and coriander. Serve with the avocado salsa.

Try this: FOR AN ALTERNATIVE: 192   FOR ENTERTAINING: 194

Pumpkin & Chickpea Curry

SERVES 4

z1 tbsp vegetable oil
1 small onion, peeled
   and sliced
2 garlic cloves, peeled
   and finely chopped
2.5 cm/1 inch piece root
   ginger, peeled and grated
1 tsp ground coriander
½ tsp ground cumin
½ tsp ground turmeric

¼ tsp ground cinnamon
2 tomatoes, chopped
2 red bird's eye
   chillies, deseeded
   and finely chopped
450 g/1 lb pumpkin
   or butternut squash
   flesh, cubed
1 tbsp hot curry paste
300 ml/½ pint vegetable

stock
1 large firm banana
400 g can chickpeas, drained
   and rinsed
salt and freshly ground
   black pepper
1 tbsp freshly
   chopped coriander
coriander sprigs, to garnish
rice or naan bread, to serve

Heat 1 tablespoon of the oil in a saucepan and add the onion. Fry gently for 5 minutes until softened. Add the garlic, ginger and spices and fry for a further minute. Add the chopped tomatoes and chillies and cook for another minute.

Add the pumpkin and curry paste and fry gently for 3–4 minutes before adding the stock. Stir well, bring to the boil and simmer for 20 minutes until the pumpkin is tender.

Thickly slice the banana and add to the pumpkin along with the chickpeas. Simmer for a further 5 minutes.

Season to taste with salt and pepper and add the chopped coriander. Serve immediately, garnished with coriander sprigs and some rice or naan bread.

Try this: FOR AN ALTERNATIVE: 242   FOR ENTERTAINING: 310

Roasted Mixed Vegetables with Garlic & Herb Sauce

SERVES 4

1 large garlic bulb
1 large onion, peeled
 and cut into wedges
4 small carrots, peeled
 and quartered
4 small parsnips, peeled
6 small potatoes, scrubbed

 and halved
1 fennel bulb, sliced thickly
4 sprigs of fresh rosemary
4 sprigs of fresh thyme
2 tbsp olive oil
salt and freshly ground
 black pepper

200 g/7 oz soft cheese
 with herbs and garlic
4 tbsp milk
zest of ½ lemon
sprigs of thyme, to garnish

Preheat the oven to 220°C/425°F/Gas Mark 7. Cut the garlic in half horizontally. Put into a large roasting tin with all the vegetables and herbs. Add the oil, season well with salt and pepper and toss together to coat lightly in the oil.

Cover with tinfoil and roast in the preheated oven for 50 minutes. Remove the tinfoil and cook for a further 30 minutes until all the vegetables are tender and slightly charred. Remove the tin from the oven and allow to cool.

In a small saucepan, melt the soft cheese together with the milk and lemon zest. Remove the garlic from the roasting tin and squeeze the flesh into a bowl. Mash thoroughly then add to the sauce. Heat through gently.

Season the vegetables to taste. Pour some sauce into small ramekins and garnish with 4 sprigs of thyme. Serve immediately with the roasted vegetables and the sauce to dip.

Try this: FOR AN ALTERNATIVE: 178 FOR ENTERTAINING: 190

Roasted Butternut Squash

SERVES 4

2 small butternut squash
4 garlic cloves, peeled
  and crushed
1 tbsp olive oil
salt and freshly ground
  black pepper
1 tbsp walnut oil
4 medium-sized leeks,
  trimmed, cleaned and

thinly sliced
1 tbsp black mustard seeds
300 g can cannellini beans,
  drained and rinsed
125 g/4 oz fine French
  beans, halved
150 ml/¼ pint vegetable
  stock
50 g/2 oz rocket

2 tbsp freshly snipped
  chives
fresh chives, to garnish

To serve:
4 tbsp fromage frais
mixed salad

Preheat the oven to 200°C/400°F/Gas Mark 6. Cut the butternut squash in half lengthwise and scoop out all of the seeds. Score the squash in a diamond pattern with a sharp knife.

Mix the garlic with the olive oil and brush over the cut surfaces of the squash. Season well with salt and pepper. Put on a baking sheet and roast for 40 minutes until tender.

Heat the walnut oil in a saucepan and fry the leeks and mustard seeds for 5 minutes. Add the drained cannellini beans, French beans and vegetable stock. Bring to the boil and simmer gently for 5 minutes until the French beans are tender.

Remove from the heat and stir in the rocket and chives. Season well. Remove the squash from the oven and allow to cool for 5 minutes. Spoon in the bean mixture. Garnish with a few snipped chives and serve immediately with the fromage frais and a mixed salad.

Vegetable Cassoulet

SERVES 6

125 g/4 oz dried haricot beans, soaked overnight
2 tbsp olive oil
2 garlic cloves, peeled and chopped
225 g/8 oz baby onions, peeled and halved
2 carrots, peeled and diced
2 celery sticks, trimmed and finely chopped
1 red pepper, deseeded and chopped
175 g/6 oz mixed mushrooms, sliced
1 tbsp each freshly chopped rosemary, thyme and sage
150 ml/¼ pint red wine
4 tbsp tomato purée
1 tbsp dark soy sauce
salt and freshly ground black pepper
50 g/2 oz fresh breadcrumbs
1 tbsp freshly chopped parsley
basil sprigs, to garnish

Preheat the oven to 190°C/375°F/Gas Mark 5. Drain the haricot beans and place in a saucepan with 1.1 litres/2 pints of fresh water. Bring to the boil and boil rapidly for 10 minutes. Reduce the heat and simmer gently for 45 minutes. Drain the beans, reserving 300 ml/½ pint of the liquid.

Heat 1 tablespoon of the oil in a flameproof casserole dish and add the garlic, onions, carrot, celery and red pepper. Cook gently for 10–12 minutes until tender and starting to brown. Add a little water if the vegetables start to stick. Add the mushrooms and cook for a further 5 minutes until softened. Add the herbs and stir briefly. Stir in the red wine and boil rapidly for about 5 minutes until reduced and syrupy. Stir in the reserved beans and their liquid, tomato purée and soy sauce. Season to taste with salt and pepper.

Mix together the breadcrumbs and parsley with the remaining 1 tablespoon of oil. Scatter this mixture evenly over the top of the stew. Cover loosely with foil and transfer to the preheated oven. Cook for 30 minutes. Carefully remove the foil and cook for a further 15–20 minutes until the topping is crisp and golden. Serve immediately, garnished with basil sprigs.

Try this: FOR AN ALTERNATIVE: 262   FOR ENTERTAINING: 270

Creamy Puy Lentils

SERVES 4

225 g/8 oz puy lentils
1 tbsp olive oil
1 garlic clove, peeled and
   finely chopped
zest and juice of 1 lemon
1 tsp wholegrain mustard
1 tbsp freshly

chopped tarragon
3 tbsp crème fraîche
salt and freshly ground
   black pepper
2 small tomatoes, deseeded
   and chopped
50 g/2 oz pitted black olives

1 tbsp freshly
   chopped parsley

To garnish:
sprigs of fresh tarragon
lemon wedges

Put the lentils in a saucepan with plenty of cold water and bring to the boil. Boil rapidly for 10 minutes, reduce the heat and simmer gently for a further 20 minutes until just tender. Drain well.

Meanwhile, prepare the dressing. Heat the oil in a frying pan over a medium heat. Add the garlic and cook for about a minute until just beginning to brown. Add the lemon zest and juice.

Add the mustard and cook for a further 30 seconds. Add the tarragon and crème fraîche and season to taste with salt and pepper.

Simmer and add the drained lentils, tomatoes and olives. Transfer to a serving dish and sprinkle the chopped parsley on top.

Garnish the lentils with the tarragon sprigs and the lemon wedges and serve immediately.

Try this: FOR AN ALTERNATIVE: 184   FOR ENTERTAINING: 242

Peperonata

SERVES 6

2 red peppers
2 yellow peppers
450 g/1 lb waxy potatoes
1 large onion
2 tbsp good quality virgin
   olive oil

700 g/1½ lb tomatoes,
   peeled, deseeded
   and chopped
2 small courgettes
50 g/2 oz pitted black
   olives, quartered

small handful basil leaves
salt and freshly ground
   black pepper
crusty bread, to serve

Prepare the peppers by halving them lengthwise and removing the stems, seeds, and membranes.

Cut the peppers lengthwise into strips about 1 cm/½ inch wide. Peel the potatoes and cut into rough dice, about 2.5–3 cm/1–1¼ inch across. Cut the onion lengthwise into eight wedges.

Heat the olive oil in a large saucepan over a medium heat. Add the onion and cook for about 5 minutes, or until starting to brown.

Add the peppers, potatoes, tomatoes, courgettes, black olives and about four torn basil leaves. Season to taste with salt and pepper.

Stir the mixture, cover and cook over a very low heat for about 40 minutes, or until the vegetables are tender but still hold their shape. Garnish with the remaining basil. Transfer to a serving bowl and serve immediately, with chunks of crusty bread.

Try this: FOR AN ALTERNATIVE: 188   FOR ENTERTAINING: 206

Mushroom Stew

SERVES 4

15 g/½ oz dried
   porcini mushrooms
900 g/2 lb assorted fresh
   mushrooms, wiped
2 tbsp good quality
   virgin olive oil
1 onion, peeled and
   finely chopped

2 garlic cloves, peeled and
   finely chopped
1 tbsp fresh thyme leaves
pinch of ground cloves
salt and freshly ground
   black pepper
700 g/1½ lb tomatoes,
   peeled, deseeded

   and chopped
225 g/8 oz instant polenta
600ml/1 pint vegetable stock
3 tbsp freshly chopped
   mixed herbs
sprigs of parsley, to garnish

Soak the porcini mushrooms in a small bowl of hot water for 20 minutes. Drain, reserving both the mushrooms and their soaking liquid. Cut the fresh mushrooms in half and reserve.

In a saucepan, heat the oil and add the onion. Cook gently for 5–7 minutes until softened. Add the garlic, thyme and cloves and continue cooking for 2 minutes.

Add all the mushrooms and cook for 8–10 minutes until the mushrooms have softened, stirring often. Season to taste with salt and pepper and add the tomatoes and the reserved soaking liquid.

Simmer, partly covered, over a low heat for about 20 minutes until thickened. Adjust the seasoning to taste.

Meanwhile, cook the polenta according to the packet instructions and using the vegetable stock. Stir in the herbs and divide between four dishes. Ladle the mushrooms over the polenta, garnish with the parsley and serve immediately.

Try this: FOR AN ALTERNATIVE: 220   FOR ENTERTAINING: 34

Huevos Rancheros

SERVES 4

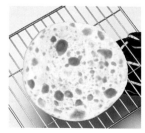

2 tbsp olive oil
1 large onion, peeled
 and finely chopped
1 red pepper, deseeded
 and finely chopped
2 garlic cloves, peeled
 and finely chopped
2–4 green chillies, deseeded
 and finely chopped

1 tsp ground cumin
1 tsp chilli powder
2 tsp ground coriander
2 tbsp freshly
 chopped coriander
700 g/1½ lb ripe plum
 tomatoes, peeled,
 deseeded and roughly
 chopped

¼ tsp sugar
8 small eggs
4–8 flour tortillas
salt and freshly ground
 black pepper
sprigs of fresh coriander,
 to garnish
refried beans, to
 serve (optional)

Heat the oil in a large, heavy-based saucepan. Add the onion and pepper and cook over a medium heat for 10 minutes. Add the garlic, chillies, ground cumin, chilli powder and chopped coriander and cook for a further minute.

Add the tomatoes and sugar. Stir well, cover and cook gently for 20 minutes. Uncover and cook for a further 20 minutes.

Lightly poach the eggs in a large frying pan, filled with gently simmering water. Drain well and keep warm. Place the tortillas briefly under a preheated hot grill. Turn once, then remove from the grill when crisp.

Add the freshly chopped coriander to the tomato sauce and season to taste with salt and pepper.

To serve, arrange two tortillas on each serving plate, top with two eggs and spoon the sauce over. Garnish with sprigs of fresh coriander and serve immediately with warmed refried beans, if liked.

Try this: FOR AN ALTERNATIVE: 220   FOR ENTERTAINING: 360

Bulghur Wheat Salad with Minty Lemon Dressing

SERVES 4

125 g/4 oz bulghur wheat
10 cm/4 inch piece
  cucumber
2 shallots, peeled
125 g/4 oz baby sweetcorn
3 ripe but firm tomatoes

For the dressing:
grated rind of 1 lemon
3 tbsp lemon juice
3 tbsp freshly chopped mint
2 tbsp freshly chopped
  parsley

1–2 tsp clear honey
2 tbsp sunflower oil
salt and freshly ground
  black pepper

Place the bulghur wheat in a saucepan and cover with boiling water. Simmer for about 10 minutes, then drain thoroughly and turn into a serving bowl.

Cut the cucumber into small dice, chop the shallots finely and reserve. Steam the sweetcorn over a pan of boiling water for 10 minutes or until tender. Drain and slice into thick chunks.

Cut a cross on the top of each tomato and place in boiling water until their skins start to peel away. Remove the skins and the seeds and cut the tomatoes into small dice.

Make the dressing by briskly whisking all the ingredients in a small bowl until mixed well.

When the bulghur wheat has cooled a little, add all the prepared vegetables and stir in the dressing. Season to taste with salt and pepper and serve.

Carrot & Parsnip Terrine

SERVES 8-10

550 g/1¼ lb carrots, peeled and chopped
450 g/1 lb parsnips, peeled and chopped
6 tbsp crème fraîche
450 g/1 lb spinach, rinsed
1 tbsp brown sugar

1 tbsp freshly chopped parsley
½ tsp freshly grated nutmeg
salt and freshly ground black pepper
6 medium eggs
sprigs of fresh basil,

to garnish

For the tomato coulis:
450 g/1 lb ripe tomatoes, deseeded and chopped
1 medium onion, peeled and finely chopped

Preheat the oven to 200°C/400°F/Gas Mark 6. Oil and line a 900 g/2 lb loaf tin with non-stick baking paper. Cook the carrots and parsnips in boiling salted water for 10–15 minutes or until very tender. Drain and purée separately. Add 2 tablespoons of crème fraîche to both the carrots and the parsnips. Steam the spinach for 5–10 minutes or until very tender. Drain and squeeze out as much liquid as possible, then stir in the remaining crème fraîche. Add the brown sugar to the carrot purée, the parsley to the parsnip mixture and the nutmeg to the spinach. Season all to taste with salt and pepper.

Beat 2 eggs, add to the spinach and turn into the prepared tin. Add another 2 beaten eggs to the carrot mixture and layer carefully on top of the spinach. Beat the remaining eggs into the parsnip purée and layer on top of the terrine. Place the tin in a baking dish and pour in enough hot water to come halfway up the sides of the tin. Bake in the preheated oven for 1 hour until a skewer inserted into the centre comes out clean. Leave the terrine to cool for at least 30 minutes. Run a sharp knife around the edges. Turn out on to a dish and reserve.

Make the tomato coulis by simmering the tomatoes and onions together for 5–10 minutes until slightly thickened. Season to taste. Blend well in a liquidiser or food processor and serve as an accompaniment to the terrine. Garnish with sprigs of basil and serve.

Try this: FOR AN ALTERNATIVE: 170 FOR ENTERTAINING: 210

Hot & Spicy Red Cabbage with Apples

SERVES 8

900 g/2 lb red cabbage, cored and shredded
450 g/1 lb onions, peeled and finely sliced
450 g/1 lb cooking apples, peeled, cored and finely sliced

½ tsp mixed spice
1 tsp ground cinnamon
2 tbsp light soft brown sugar
salt and freshly ground black pepper
grated rind of 1 large orange
1 tbsp fresh orange juice

50 ml/2 fl oz medium sweet cider (or apple juice)
2 tbsp wine vinegar

To serve:
crème fraîche
freshly ground black pepper

Preheat the oven to 150°C/300°F/Gas Mark 2. Put just enough cabbage in a large casserole dish to cover the base evenly.

Place a layer of the onions and apples on top of the cabbage. Sprinkle a little of the mixed spice, cinnamon and sugar over the top. Season with salt and pepper.

Spoon over a small portion of the orange rind, orange juice and the cider. Continue to layer the casserole dish with the ingredients in the same order until used up. Pour the vinegar as evenly as possible over the top layer of the ingredients.

Cover the casserole dish with a close-fitting lid and bake in the preheated oven, stirring occasionally, for 2 hours until the cabbage is moist and tender. Serve immediately with the crème fraîche and black pepper.

Try this: FOR AN ALTERNATIVE: 178   FOR ENTERTAINING: 196

Marinated Vegetable Kebabs

SERVES 4

2 small courgettes, cut into
  2 cm/¾ inch pieces
½ green pepper, deseeded
  and cut into 2.5 cm/1 inch
  pieces
½ red pepper, deseeded and
  cut into 2.5 cm/1 inch
  pieces
½ yellow pepper, deseeded
  and cut into 2.5 cm/
  1 inch pieces

8 baby onions, peeled
8 button mushrooms
8 cherry tomatoes
freshly chopped parsley,
  to garnish
freshly cooked couscous,
  to serve

For the marinade:
1 tbsp light olive oil
4 tbsp dry sherry

2 tbsp light soy sauce
1 red chilli, deseeded and
  finely chopped
2 garlic cloves, peeled
  and crushed
2.5 cm/1 inch piece root
  ginger, peeled and
  finely grated

Place the courgettes, peppers and baby onions in a pan of just boiled water. Bring back to the boil and simmer for about 30 seconds. Drain and rinse the cooked vegetables in cold water and dry on absorbent kitchen paper.

Thread the cooked vegetables and the mushrooms and tomatoes alternately on to skewers and place in a large shallow dish.

Make the marinade by whisking all the ingredients together until thoroughly blended. Pour the marinade evenly over the kebabs, then chill in the refrigerator for at least 1 hour. Spoon the marinade over the kebabs occasionally during this time.

Place the kebabs in a hot griddle pan or on a hot barbecue and cook gently for 10–12 minutes. Turn the kebabs frequently and brush with the marinade when needed. When the vegetables are tender, sprinkle over the chopped parsley and serve immediately with couscous.

Try this: FOR AN ALTERNATIVE: 346   FOR ENTERTAINING: 168

Pumpkin Pâté

SERVES 8-10

450 g/1 lb fresh pumpkin flesh (when in season), peeled, or 425 g can pumpkin purée
1 tsp sunflower oil
1 small onion, peeled and finely chopped
½ orange pepper, deseeded and finely chopped
2 medium eggs, beaten
3 tbsp natural yogurt
125 g/4 oz hard cheese (such as Edam, Cheddar or Gouda cheese), grated
50 g/2 oz wheatgerm
1 tbsp freshly chopped oregano
salt and freshly ground black pepper
fresh salad leaves and crusty bread, to serve

Preheat the oven to 180°C/350°F/Gas Mark 4. Oil and line a 900 ml/1½ pint oblong dish or loaf tin. Cut the pumpkin flesh into cubes and place in a pan of boiling water. Simmer for 20 minutes or until the pumpkin is very tender. Drain and leave to cool, then mash well to form a purée.

Heat the oil in a non-stick frying pan and cook the chopped onion and pepper for about 4 minutes, until softened.

Mix together the puréed pumpkin, softened vegetables, eggs and yogurt. Add the cheese, wheatgerm and chopped oregano. Season well with salt and pepper.

When the pumpkin mixture is well blended, spoon it into the prepared tin and stand in a baking dish. Fill the tray with hot water to come halfway up the sides of the tin and carefully place in the preheated oven.

Bake for about 1 hour or until firm, then leave to cool. Chill for 30 minutes before turning out on to a serving plate. Serve with crusty bread and a fresh salad.

Spanish Baked Tomatoes

SERVES 4

175 g/6 oz whole-grain rice
600 ml/1 pint vegetable
   stock
2 tsp sunflower oil
2 shallots, peeled and
   finely chopped
1 garlic clove, peeled
   and crushed

1 green pepper, deseeded
   and cut into small dice
1 red chilli, deseeded and
   finely chopped
50 g/2 oz button mushrooms
   finely chopped
1 tbsp freshly
   chopped oregano

salt and freshly ground
   black pepper
4 large ripe beef tomatoes
1 large egg, beaten
1 tsp caster sugar
basil leaves, to garnish
crusty bread, to serve

Preheat the oven to 180°C/350°F/Gas Mark 4. Place the rice in a saucepan, pour over the vegetable stock and bring to the boil. Simmer for 30 minutes or until the rice is tender. Drain and turn into a mixing bowl.

Add 1 teaspoon of sunflower oil to a small, non-stick pan and gently fry the shallots, garlic, pepper, chilli and mushrooms for 2 minutes. Add to the rice with the chopped oregano. Season with plenty of salt and pepper.

Slice the top off each tomato. Cut and scoop out the flesh, removing the hard core. Pass the tomato flesh through a sieve. Add 1 tablespoon of the juice to the rice mixture. Stir in the beaten egg and mix. Sprinkle a little sugar in the base of each tomato. Pile the rice mixture into the shells.

Place the tomatoes in a baking dish and pour a little cold water around them. Replace their lids and drizzle a few drops of sunflower oil over the tops. Bake in the preheated oven for about 25 minutes. Garnish with the basil leaves and season with black pepper and serve immediately with crusty bread.

Try this: FOR AN ALTERNATIVE: 296   FOR ENTERTAINING: 214

Stuffed Onions with Pine Nuts

SERVES 4

4 medium onions, peeled
2 garlic cloves, peeled
   and crushed
2 tbsp fresh
   brown breadcrumbs
2 tbsp white breadcrumbs

25 g/1 oz sultanas
25 g/1 oz pine nuts
50 g/2 oz hard cheese
   such as Edam or
   Cheddar, grated
2 tbsp freshly chopped

parsley
1 medium egg, beaten
salt and freshly ground
   black pepper
salad leaves, to serve

Preheat the oven to 200°C/400°F/Gas Mark 6. Bring a pan of water to the boil, add the onions and cook gently for about 15 minutes.

Drain well. Allow the onions to cool, then slice each one in half horizontally. Scoop out most of the onion flesh but leave a reasonably firm shell.

Chop up 4 tablespoons of the onion flesh and place in a bowl with the crushed garlic, breadcrumbs, sultanas, pine nuts, grated cheese and parsley.

Mix the breadcrumb mixture together thoroughly. Bind together with as much of the beaten egg as necessary to make a firm filling. Season to taste with salt and pepper.

Pile the mixture back into the onion shells and top with the grated cheese. Place on a oiled baking tray and cook in the preheated oven for 20–30 minutes or until golden brown. Serve immediately with the salad leaves.

Try this: FOR AN ALTERNATIVE: 230 FOR ENTERTAINING: 272

Warm Leek & Tomato Salad

SERVES 4

450 g/1 lb trimmed
  baby leeks
225 g/8 oz ripe, but
  firm tomatoes
2 shallots, peeled and cut
  into thin wedges

For the honey &
  lime dressing:
2 tbsp clear honey
grated rind of 1 lime
4 tbsp lime juice
1 tbsp light olive oil

1 tsp Dijon mustard
salt and freshly ground
  black pepper
To garnish:
freshly chopped tarragon
freshly chopped basil

Trim the leeks so that they are all the same length. Place in a steamer over a pan of boiling water and steam for 8 minutes or until just tender. Drain the leeks thoroughly and arrange in a shallow serving dish.

Make a cross in the top of the tomatoes, place in a bowl and cover them with boiling water until their skins start to peel away. Remove from the bowl and carefully remove the skins.

Cut the tomatoes into four and remove the seeds, then chop into small dice. Spoon over the top of the leeks together with the shallots.

In a small bowl make the dressing by whisking the honey, lime rind, lime juice, olive oil, mustard and salt and pepper. Pour 3 tablespoons of the dressing over the leeks and tomatoes and garnish with the tarragon and basil. Serve while the leeks are still warm, with the remaining dressing served separately.

Try this: FOR AN ALTERNATIVE: 222   FOR ENTERTAINING: 196

Beetroot & Potato Medley

SERVES 4

350 g/12 oz raw
   baby beetroot
½ tsp sunflower oil
225 g/8 oz new potatoes
½ cucumber, peeled

3 tbsp white wine vinegar
150 ml/5 fl oz natural
   yogurt
salt and freshly ground
   black pepper

fresh salad leaves
1 tbsp freshly snipped
   chives, to garnish

Preheat the oven to 180°C/350°F/Gas Mark 4. Scrub the beetroot thoroughly and place on a baking tray. Brush the beetroot with a little oil and cook for 1½ hours or until a skewer is easily insertable into the beetroot. Allow to cool a little, then remove the skins.

Cook the potatoes in boiling water for about 10 minutes. Rinse in cold water and drain. Reserve the potatoes until cool. Dice evenly.

Cut the cucumber into cubes and place in a mixing bowl. Chop the beetroot into small cubes and add to the bowl with the reserved potatoes. Gently mix the vegetables together.

Mix together the vinegar and yogurt and season to taste with a little salt and pepper. Pour over the vegetables and combine gently.

Arrange on a bed of salad leaves garnished with the snipped chives and serve.

Try this: FOR AN ALTERNATIVE: 176   FOR ENTERTAINING: 120

Light Ratatouille

SERVES 4

1 red pepper
2 courgettes, trimmed
1 small aubergine, trimmed
1 onion, peeled

2 ripe tomatoes
50 g/2 oz button
   mushrooms, wiped
   and halved or quartered

200 ml/7 fl oz tomato juice
1 tbsp freshly chopped basil
salt and freshly ground
   black pepper

De-seed the peppers, remove the membrane with a small sharp knife and cut into small dice. Thickly slice the courgettes and cut the aubergine into small dice. Slice the onion into rings.

Place the tomatoes in boiling water until their skins begin to peel away. Remove the skins from the tomatoes, cut into quarters and remove the seeds.

Place all the vegetables in a saucepan with the tomato juice and basil. Season to taste with salt and pepper. Bring to the boil, cover and simmer for 15 minutes or until the vegetables are tender. Remove the vegetables with a slotted spoon and arrange in a serving dish.

Bring the liquid in the pan to the boil and boil for 20 seconds until it is slightly thickened. Season the sauce to taste with salt and pepper.

Pass the sauce through a sieve to remove some of the seeds and pour over the vegetables. Serve the ratatouille hot or cold.

Try this: FOR AN ALTERNATIVE: 320 FOR ENTERTAINING: 232

Sicilian Baked Aubergine

SERVES 4

1 large aubergine, trimmed
2 celery stalks, trimmed
4 large ripe tomatoes
1 tsp sunflower oil
2 shallots, peeled and
    finely chopped

1½ tsp tomato purée
25 g/1 oz green pitted olives
25 g/1 oz black pitted olives
salt and freshly ground
    black pepper
1 tbsp white wine vinegar

2 tsp caster sugar
1 tbsp freshly chopped basil,
    to garnish
mixed salad leaves, to serve

Preheat the oven to 200°C/400°F/Gas Mark 6. Cut the aubergine into small cubes and place on an oiled baking tray. Cover the tray with tinfoil and bake in the preheated oven for 15–20 minutes until soft. Reserve, to allow the aubergine to cool.

Place the celery and tomatoes in a large bowl and cover with boiling water. Remove the tomatoes from the bowl when their skins begin to peel away. Remove the skins then, deseed and chop the flesh into small pieces. Remove the celery from the bowl of water, finely chop and reserve.

Pour the vegetable oil into a non-stick saucepan, add the chopped shallots and fry gently for 2–3 minutes until soft. Add the celery, tomatoes, tomato purée and olives. Season to taste with salt and pepper.

Simmer gently for 3–4 minutes. Add the vinegar, sugar and cooled aubergine to the pan and heat gently for 2–3 minutes until all the ingredients are well blended. Reserve to allow the aubergine mixture to cool. When cool, garnish with the chopped basil and serve cold with salad leaves.

Try this: FOR AN ALTERNATIVE: 216   FOR ENTERTAINING: 242

Pasta with Raw Fennel, Tomato & Red Onions

SERVES 6

1 fennel bulb
700 g/1½ lb tomatoes
1 garlic clove
¼ small red onion
small handful fresh basil

small handful fresh mint
100 ml/3½ fl oz extra virgin
   olive oil, plus extra to serve
juice of 1 lemon
salt and freshly ground

black pepper
450 g/1 lb penne or pennette
freshly grated
   Parmesan cheese,
   to serve

Trim the fennel and slice thinly. Stack the slices and cut into sticks, then cut crosswise again into fine dice. De-seed the tomatoes and chop them finely. Peel and finely chop or crush the garlic. Peel and finely chop or grate the onion.

Stack the basil leaves then roll up tightly. Slice crosswise into fine shreds. Finely chop the mint. Place the chopped vegetables and herbs in a medium-sized bowl. Add the olive oil and lemon juice and mix together. Season well with salt and pepper then leave for 30 minutes to allow the flavours to develop.

Bring a large pan of salted water to a rolling boil. Add the pasta and cook according to the packet instructions, or until 'al dente'.

Drain the cooked pasta thoroughly. Transfer to a warmed serving dish, pour over the vegetable mixture and toss. Serve with the grated Parmesan cheese and extra olive oil to drizzle over.

Try this: FOR AN ALTERNATIVE: 112   FOR ENTERTAINING: 260

Vegetarian Cassoulet

SERVES 4

225 g/8 oz dried haricot
beans, soaked overnight
2 medium onions
1 bay leaf
1.4 litres/2½ pints cold water
550 g/1¼ lb large potatoes,
peeled and cut into 1 cm/
½ inch slices
salt and freshly ground
black pepper

5 tsp olive oil
1 large garlic clove,
peeled and crushed
2 leeks, trimmed and sliced
200 g can chopped tomatoes
1 tsp dark muscovado sugar
1 tbsp freshly
chopped thyme
2 tbsp freshly
chopped parsley

3 courgettes, trimmed
and sliced

For the topping:
50 g/2 oz fresh white
breadcrumbs
25 g/1oz Cheddar cheese,
finely grated

Preheat the oven to 180°C/350°F/Gas Mark 4, 10 minutes before required. Drain the beans, rinse under cold running water and put in a saucepan. Peel 1 of the onions and add to the beans with the bay leaf. Pour in the water. Bring to a rapid boil and cook for 10 minutes, then turn down the heat, cover and simmer for 50 minutes, or until the beans are almost tender. Drain the beans, reserving the liquor, but discarding the onion and bay leaf.

Cook the potatoes in a saucepan of lightly salted boiling water for 6–7 minutes until almost tender when tested with the point of a knife. Drain and reserve. Peel and chop the remaining onion. Heat the oil in a frying pan and cook the onion with the garlic and leeks for 10 minutes until softened. Stir in the tomatoes, sugar, thyme and parsley. Stir in the beans, with 300 ml/½ pint of the reserved liquor and season to taste. Simmer, uncovered, for 5 minutes.

Layer the potato slices, courgettes and ladlefuls of the bean mixture in a large flameproof casserole dish. To make the topping, mix together the breadcrumbs and cheese and sprinkle over the top. Bake in the preheated oven for 40 minutes, or until the vegetables are cooked through and the topping is golden brown and crisp. Serve immediately.

 Try this: FOR AN ALTERNATIVE: 306   FOR ENTERTAINING: 262

Sweet Potato Cakes with Mango & Tomato Salsa

SERVES 4

700 g/1½ lb sweet potatoes, peeled and cut into large chunks
salt and freshly ground black pepper
25 g/1 oz butter
1 onion, peeled and chopped
1 garlic clove, peeled and crushed

pinch of freshly grated nutmeg
1 medium egg, beaten
50 g/2 oz quick-cook polenta
2 tbsp sunflower oil

For the salsa:
1 ripe mango, peeled, stoned and diced
6 cherry tomatoes,

cut in wedges
4 spring onions, trimmed and thinly sliced
1 red chilli, deseeded and finely chopped
finely grated rind and juice of ½ lime
2 tbsp freshly chopped mint
1 tsp clear honey
salad leaves, to serve

Steam or cook the sweet potatoes in lightly salted boiling water for 15–20 minutes, until tender. Drain well, then mash until smooth.

Melt the butter in a saucepan. Add the onion and garlic and cook gently for 10 minutes until soft. Add to the mashed sweet potato and season with the nutmeg, salt and pepper. Stir together until mixed thoroughly. Leave to cool.

Shape the mixture into four oval potato cakes, about 2.5 cm/1 inch thick. Dip first in the beaten egg, allowing the excess to fall back into the bowl, then coat in the polenta. Refrigerate for at least 30 minutes.

Meanwhile, mix together all the ingredients for the salsa. Spoon into a serving bowl, cover with clingfilm and leave at room temperature to allow the flavours to develop.

Heat the oil in a frying pan and cook the potato cakes for 4–5 minutes on each side. Serve with the salsa and salad leaves.

Cheese & Onion Oat Pie

SERVES 4

1 tbsp sunflower oil,
  plus 1 tsp extra
25 g/1 oz butter
2 medium onions, peeled
  and sliced
1 garlic clove, peeled

  and crushed
150 g/5 oz porridge oats
125 g/4 oz mature Cheddar
  cheese, grated
2 medium eggs,
  lightly beaten

2 tbsp freshly
  chopped parsley
salt and freshly
  ground black pepper
275 g/10 oz baking
  potato, peeled

Preheat the oven to 180˚C/350˚F/Gas Mark 4. Heat the oil and half the butter in a saucepan until melted. Add the onions and garlic and gently cook for 10 minutes, or until soft. Remove from the heat and tip into a large bowl.

Spread the oats out on a baking sheet and toast in the hot oven for 12 minutes. Leave to cool, then add to the onions with the cheese, eggs and parsley. Season to taste with salt and pepper and mix well.

Line the base of a 20.5 cm/8 inch round sandwich tin with greaseproof paper and oil well. Thinly slice the potato and arrange the slices on the base, overlapping them slightly.

Spoon the cheese and oat mixture on top of the potato, spreading evenly with the back of a spoon. Cover with tinfoil and bake for 30 minutes. Invert the pie onto a baking sheet so that the potatoes are on top. Carefully remove the tin and lining paper.

Preheat the grill to medium. Melt the remaining butter and carefully brush over the potato topping. Cook under the preheated grill for 5–6 minutes until the potatoes are lightly browned. Cut into wedges and serve.

Try this: FOR AN ALTERNATIVE: 286   FOR ENTERTAINING: 164

Chunky Vegetable & Fennel Goulash with Dumplings

SERVES 4

2 fennel bulbs, weighing about 450 g/1 lb
2 tbsp sunflower oil
1 large onion, peeled and sliced
1½ tbsp paprika
1 tbsp plain flour
300 ml/½ pint vegetable stock
400 g can chopped tomatoes

450 g/1 lb potatoes, peeled and cut into 2.5 cm/1 inch chunks
125 g/4 oz small button mushrooms
salt and freshly ground black pepper

For the dumplings:
1 tbsp sunflower oil

1 small onion, peeled and finely chopped
1 medium egg
3 tbsp milk
3 tbsp freshly chopped parsley
125 g/4 oz fresh white breadcrumbs

Cut the fennel bulbs in half widthways. Thickly slice the stalks and cut the bulbs into eight wedges. Heat the oil in a large saucepan or flameproof casserole. Add the onion and fennel and cook gently for 10 minutes until soft. Stir in the paprika and flour.

Remove from the heat and gradually stir in the stock. Add the chopped tomatoes, potatoes and mushrooms. Season to taste with salt and pepper. Bring to the boil, reduce the heat and simmer for 20 minutes.

Meanwhile, make the dumplings. Heat the oil in a frying pan and gently cook the onion for 10 minutes, until soft. Leave to cool for a few minutes.

In a bowl, beat the egg and milk together, then add the onion, parsley, breadcrumbs, and season to taste. With damp hands form the breadcrumb mixture into 12 round dumplings each about the size of a walnut. Arrange the dumplings on top of the goulash. Cover and cook for a further 15 minutes, until the dumplings are cooked and the vegetables are tender. Serve immediately.

Try this: FOR AN ALTERNATIVE: 192   FOR ENTERTAINING: 184

Cabbage Timbale

SERVES 4-6

1 small savoy cabbage,
   weighing about
   350 g/12 oz
salt and freshly ground
   black pepper
2 tbsp olive oil
1 leek, trimmed and
   chopped

1 garlic clove, peeled
   and crushed
75 g/3 oz long-grain rice
200 g can chopped tomatoes
300 ml/½ pint
   vegetable stock
400 g can flageolet beans,
   drained and rinsed

75 g/3 oz Cheddar
   cheese, grated
1 tbsp freshly chopped
   oregano

To garnish:
Greek yogurt with paprika
tomato wedges

Preheat the oven to 180°C/350°F/Gas Mark 4, 10 minutes before required. Remove six of the outer leaves of the cabbage. Cut off the thickest part of the stalk and blanch the leaves in lightly salted boiling water for 2 minutes. Lift out with a slotted spoon and briefly rinse under cold water and reserve. Remove the stalks from the rest of the cabbage leaves. Shred the leaves and blanch in the boiling water for 1 minute. Drain, rinse under cold water and pat dry on absorbent kitchen paper.

Heat the oil in a frying pan and cook the leek and garlic for 5 minutes. Stir in the rice, chopped tomatoes with their juice and stock. Bring to the boil, cover and simmer for 15 minutes. Remove the lid and simmer for a further 4–5 minutes, stirring frequently, until the liquid is absorbed and the rice is tender. Stir in the flageolet beans, cheese and oregano. Season to taste with salt and pepper.

Line an oiled 1.1 litre/2 pint pudding basin with some of the large cabbage leaves, over-lapping them slightly. Fill the basin with alternate layers of rice mixture and shredded leaves, pressing down well. Cover the top with the remaining leaves. Cover with oiled tinfoil and bake in the preheated for 30 minutes. Leave to stand for 10 minutes. Turn out, cut into wedges and serve with yogurt sprinkled with paprika and tomato wedges.

 Try this: FOR AN ALTERNATIVE: 78   FOR ENTERTAINING: 274

Layered Cheese & Herb Potato Cake

SERVES 4

900 g/2 lb waxy potatoes
3 tbsp freshly
    snipped chives
2 tbsp freshly
    chopped parsley
225 g/8 oz mature
    Cheddar cheese

2 large egg yolks
1 tsp paprika
125 g/4 oz fresh white
    breadcrumbs
50 g/2 oz almonds,
    toasted and
    roughly chopped

50 g/2 oz butter, melted
salt and freshly ground
    black pepper
mixed salad or steamed
    vegetables, to serve

Preheat the oven to 180°C/350°F/Gas Mark 4. Lightly oil and line the base of a 20.5 cm/ 8 inch round cake tin with lightly oiled greaseproof or baking parchment paper. Peel and thinly slice the potatoes and reserve. Stir the chives, parsley, cheese and egg yolks together in a small bowl and reserve. Mix the paprika into the breadcrumbs.

Sprinkle the almonds over the base of the lined tin. Cover with half the potatoes, arranging them in layers, then sprinkle with the paprika bread-crumb mixture and season to taste with salt and pepper.

Spoon the cheese and herb mixture over the breadcrumbs with a little more seasoning, then arrange the remaining potatoes on top. Drizzle over the melted butter and press the surface down firmly.

Bake in the preheated oven for 1¼ hours, or until golden and cooked through. Let the tin stand for 10 minutes before carefully turning out and serving in thick wedges. Serve immediately with salad or freshly cooked vegetables.

Try this: FOR AN ALTERNATIVE: 230   FOR ENTERTAINING: 82

Rice Nuggets in Herby Tomato Sauce

SERVES 4

600 ml/1 pint vegetable stock	2 tbsp freshly chopped parsley	1 onion, peeled and thinly sliced
1 bay leaf	salt and freshly ground black pepper	1 garlic clove, peeled and crushed
175 g/6 oz Arborio rice	grated Parmesan cheese, to serve	1 small yellow pepper, deseeded and diced
50 g/2 oz Cheddar cheese, grated	For the herby tomato sauce:	400 g can chopped tomatoes
1 medium egg yolk	1 tbsp olive oil	1 tbsp freshly chopped basil
1 tbsp plain flour		

Pour the stock into a large saucepan. Add the bay leaf. Bring to the boil, add the rice, stir, then cover and simmer for 15 minutes. Uncover, reduce the heat to low and cook for a further 5 minutes until the rice is tender and all the stock is absorbed, stirring frequently towards the end of cooking time. Cool.

Stir the cheese, egg yolk, flour and parsley into the rice. Season to taste, then shape into 20 walnut-sized balls. Cover and refrigerate.

To make the sauce, heat the oil in a large frying pan and cook the onion for 5 minutes. Add the garlic and yellow pepper and cook for a further 5 minutes, until soft. Stir in the chopped tomatoes and simmer gently for 3 minutes. Stir in the chopped basil and season to taste.

Add the rice nuggets to the sauce and simmer for a further 10 minutes, or until the rice nuggets are cooked through and the sauce has reduced a little. Spoon onto serving plates and serve hot, sprinkled with grated Parmesan cheese.

Try this: FOR AN ALTERNATIVE: 232   FOR ENTERTAINING: 64

Mixed Grain Pilaf

SERVES 4

2 tbsp olive oil
1 garlic clove, peeled
and crushed
½ tsp ground turmeric
125 g/4 oz mixed long-grain
and wild rice
50 g/2 oz red lentils
300 ml/½ pint vegetable
stock

200 g can chopped tomatoes
5 cm/2 inch piece
cinnamon stick
salt and freshly ground
black pepper
400 g can mixed beans,
drained and rinsed
15 g/½ oz butter
1 bunch spring onions,

trimmed and finely sliced
3 medium eggs
4 tbsp freshly chopped
herbs, such as parsley
and chervil
sprigs of fresh dill,
to garnish

Heat 1 tablespoon of the oil in a saucepan. Add the garlic and turmeric and cook for a few seconds. Stir in the rice and lentils. Add the stock, tomatoes and cinnamon. Season to taste with salt and pepper. Stir once and bring to the boil. Lower the heat, cover and simmer for 20 minutes, until most of the stock is absorbed and the rice and lentils are tender. Stir in the beans, replace the lid and leave to stand for 2–3 minutes to allow the beans to heat through.

While the rice is cooking, heat the remaining oil and butter in a frying pan. Add the spring onions and cook for 4–5 minutes, until soft. Lightly beat the eggs with 2 tablespoons of the herbs, then season with salt and pepper.

Pour the egg mixture over the spring onions. Stir gently with a spatula over a low heat, drawing the mixture from the sides to the centre as the omelette sets. When almost set, stop stirring and cook for about 30 seconds until golden underneath.

Remove the omelette from the pan, roll up and slice into thin strips. Fluff the rice up with a fork and remove the cinnamon stick. Spoon onto serving plates, top with strips of omelette and the remaining chopped herbs. Garnish with sprigs of dill and serve.

Try this: FOR AN ALTERNATIVE: 80   FOR ENTERTAINING: 376

Red Lentil Kedgeree with Avocado & Tomatoes

SERVES 4

150 g/5 oz basmati rice
150 g/5 oz red lentils
15 g/½ oz butter
1 tbsp sunflower oil
1 medium onion,
    peeled and chopped
1 tsp ground cumin
4 cardamom pods, bruised

1 bay leaf
450 ml/¾ pint vegetable
    stock
1 ripe avocado, peeled,
    stoned and diced
1 tbsp lemon juice
4 plum tomatoes, peeled
    and diced

2 tbsp freshly chopped
    coriander
salt and freshly ground
    black pepper
lemon or lime slices, to
    garnish

Put the rice and lentils in a sieve and rinse under cold running water. Tip into a bowl, then pour over enough cold water to cover and leave to soak for 10 minutes.

Heat the butter and oil in a saucepan. Add the sliced onion and cook gently, stirring occasionally, for 10 minutes until softened. Stir in the cumin, cardamon pods and bay leaf and cook for a further minute, stirring all the time.

Drain the rice and lentils, rinse again and add to the onions in the saucepan. Stir in the vegetable stock and bring to the boil. Reduce the heat, cover the saucepan and simmer for 14–15 minutes, or until the rice and lentils are tender.

Place the diced avocado in a bowl and toss with the lemon juice. Stir in the tomatoes and chopped coriander. Season to taste with salt and pepper.

Fluff up the rice with a fork, spoon into a warmed serving dish and spoon the avocado mixture on top. Garnish with lemon or lime slices and serve.

Try this: FOR AN ALTERNATIVE: 194 FOR ENTERTAINING: 244

Aduki Bean & Rice Burgers

SERVES 4

2½ tbsp sunflower oil
1 medium onion, peeled and very finely chopped
1 garlic clove, peeled and crushed
1 tsp curry paste
225 g/8 oz basmati rice
400 g can aduki beans, drained and rinsed
225 ml/8 fl oz vegetable

stock
125 g/4 oz firm tofu, crumbled
1 tsp garam masala
2 tbsp freshly chopped coriander
salt and freshly ground black pepper

For the carrot raita:

2 large carrots, peeled and grated
½ cucumber, cut into tiny dice
150 ml/¼ pint Greek yogurt

To serve:
wholemeal baps
tomato slices
lettuce leaves

Heat 1 tablespoon of the oil in a saucepan and gently cook the onion for 10 minutes until soft. Add the garlic and curry paste and cook for a few more seconds. Stir in the rice and beans.

Pour in the stock, bring to the boil and simmer for 12 minutes, or until all the stock has been absorbed – do not lift the lid for the first 10 minutes of cooking. Reserve.

Lightly mash the tofu. Add to the rice mixture with the garam masala, coriander, salt and pepper. Mix. Divide the mixture into eight and shape into burgers. Chill in the refrigerator for 30 minutes.

Meanwhile, make the raita. Mix together the carrots, cucumber and Greek yogurt. Spoon into a small bowl and chill in the refrigerator until ready to serve.

Heat the remaining oil in a large frying pan. Fry the burgers, in batches if necessary, for 4–5 minutes on each side, or until lightly browned. Serve in the baps with tomato slices and lettuce. Accompany with the raita.

Try this: FOR AN ALTERNATIVE: 172   FOR ENTERTAINING: 228

Venetian–style Vegetables & Beans

SERVES 4

250 g/9 oz dried pinto beans
3 sprigs of fresh parsley
1 sprig of fresh rosemary
2 tbsp olive oil
200 g can chopped tomatoes
2 shallots, peeled

For the vegetable mixture:
1 large red onion, peeled
1 large white onion, peeled
1 medium carrot, peeled
2 sticks celery, trimmed
3 tbsp olive oil

3 bay leaves
1 tsp caster sugar
3 tbsp red wine vinegar
salt and freshly ground
    black pepper

Put the beans in a bowl, cover with plenty of cold water and leave to soak for at least 8 hours, or overnight. Drain and rinse the beans. Put in a large saucepan with 1.1 litres/2 pints cold water. Tie the parsley and rosemary in muslin and add to the beans with the olive oil. Boil rapidly for 10 minutes, then lower the heat and simmer for 20 minutes with the saucepan half covered. Stir in the tomatoes and shallots and simmer for a further 10–15 minutes, or until the beans are cooked.

Meanwhile, slice the red and white onion into rings and then finely dice the carrot and celery. Heat the olive oil in a saucepan and cook the onions over a very low heat for about 10 minutes. Add the carrot, celery and bay leaves to the saucepan and cook for a further 10 minutes, stirring frequently, until the vegetables are tender. Sprinkle with sugar, stir and cook for 1 minute.

Stir in the vinegar. Cook for 1 minute, then remove the saucepan from the heat. Drain the beans through a fine sieve, discarding all the herbs, then add the beans to the onion mixture and season well with salt and pepper. Mix gently, then tip the beans into a large serving bowl. Leave to cool, then serve at room temperature.

Try this: FOR AN ALTERNATIVE: 188   FOR ENTERTAINING: 334

Roast Butternut Squash Risotto

SERVES 4

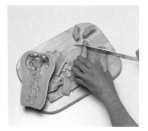

1 medium butternut squash
2 tbsp olive oil
1 garlic bulb, cloves
    separated, but unpeeled
15 g/½ oz unsalted butter
275 g/10 oz Arborio rice
large pinch of saffron
    strands

150 ml/¼ pint dry white wine
1 litre/1¾ pints vegetable
    stock
1 tbsp freshly
    chopped parsley
1 tbsp freshly
    chopped oregano
50 g/2 oz Parmesan cheese,

    finely grated
salt and freshly ground
    black pepper
sprigs of fresh oregano,
    to garnish
extra Parmesan cheese,
    to serve

Preheat the oven to 190°C/375°F/Gas Mark 5. Cut the butternut squash in half, thickly peel, then scoop out the seeds and discard. Cut the flesh into 2 cm/¾ inch cubes. Pour the oil into a large roasting tin and heat in the preheated oven for 5 minutes. Add the butternut squash and garlic cloves. Turn in the oil to coat, then roast in the oven for about 25–30 minutes, or until golden brown and very tender, turning the vegetables halfway through cooking time.

Melt the butter in a large saucepan. Add the rice and stir over a high heat for a few seconds. Add the saffron and the wine and bubble fiercely until almost totally reduced, stirring frequently. At the same time heat the stock in a separate saucepan and keep at a steady simmer. Reduce the heat under the rice to low. Add a ladleful of stock to the saucepan and simmer, stirring, until absorbed. Continue adding the stock in this way until the rice is tender. This will take about 20 minutes and it may not be necessary to add all the stock.

Turn off the heat, stir in the herbs, Parmesan cheese and seasoning. Cover and leave to stand for 2–3 minutes. Quickly remove the skins from the roasted garlic. Add to the risotto with the butternut squash and mix gently. Garnish with sprigs of oregano and serve immediately with Parmesan cheese.

Try this: FOR AN ALTERNATIVE: 190   FOR ENTERTAINING: 210

Wild Rice Dolmades

SERVES 4-6

6 tbsp olive oil
25 g/1 oz pine nuts
175 g/6 oz mushrooms,
  wiped and finely chopped
4 spring onions, trimmed
  and finely chopped
1 garlic clove, peeled

and crushed
50 g/2 oz cooked wild rice
2 tsp freshly chopped dill
2 tsp freshly chopped mint
salt and freshly ground
  black pepper
16–24 prepared medium

vine leaves
about 300 ml/½ pint
  vegetable stock

To garnish:
lemon wedges
sprigs of fresh dill

Heat 1 tbsp of the oil in a frying pan and gently cook the pine nuts for 2–3 minutes, stirring frequently, until golden. Remove from the pan and reserve.

Add 1½ tablespoons of oil to the pan and gently cook the mushrooms, spring onions and garlic for 7–8 minutes until very soft. Stir in the rice, herbs, salt and pepper.

Put a heaped teaspoon of stuffing in the centre of each leaf (if the leaves are small, put two together, overlapping slightly). Fold over the stalk end, then the sides and roll up to make a neat parcel. Continue until all the stuffing is used.

Arrange the stuffed vine leaves close together seam-side down in a large saucepan, drizzling each with a little of the remaining oil – there will be several layers. Pour over just enough stock to cover. Put an inverted plate over the dolmades to stop them unrolling during cooking. Bring to the boil, then simmer very gently for 3 minutes. Cool in the saucepan.

Transfer the dolmades to a serving dish. Cover and chill in the refrigerator before serving. Sprinkle with the pine nuts and garnish with lemon and dill. Serve.

Try this: FOR AN ALTERNATIVE: 228 FOR ENTERTAINING: 354

Mediterranean Potato Salad

SERVES 4

700 g/1½ lb small
  waxy potatoes
2 red onions, peeled and
  roughly chopped
1 yellow pepper, deseeded
  and roughly chopped
1 green pepper, deseeded
  and roughly chopped

6 tbsp extra virgin olive oil
125 g/4 oz ripe tomatoes,
  chopped
50 g/2 oz pitted black
  olives, sliced
125 g/4 oz feta cheese
3 tbsp freshly chopped
  parsley

2 tbsp white wine vinegar
1 tsp Dijon mustard
1 tsp clear honey
salt and freshly ground
  black pepper
sprigs of fresh parsley,
  to garnish

Preheat the oven to 200°C/400°F/Gas Mark 6. Place the potatoes in a large saucepan of salted water, bring to the boil and simmer until just tender. Do not overcook. Drain and plunge into cold water, to stop them from cooking further.

Place the onions in a bowl with the yellow and green peppers, then pour over 2 tablespoons of the olive oil. Stir and spoon onto a large baking tray. Cook in the preheated oven for 25–30 minutes, or until the vegetables are tender and lightly charred in places, stirring occasionally. Remove from the oven and transfer to a large bowl.

Cut the potatoes into bite-sized pieces and mix with the roasted onions and peppers. Add the tomatoes and olives to the potatoes. Crumble over the feta cheese and sprinkle with the chopped parsley.

Whisk together the remaining olive oil, vinegar, mustard and honey, then season to taste with salt and pepper. Pour the dressing over the potatoes and toss gently together. Garnish with parsley sprigs and serve immediately.

Try this: FOR AN ALTERNATIVE: 324   FOR ENTERTAINING: 74

Broad Bean & Artichoke Risotto

SERVES 4

275 g/10 oz frozen broad beans
400 g can artichoke hearts, drained
1 tbsp sunflower oil
150 ml/¼ pint dry white wine
900 ml/1½ pints vegetable

stock
25 g/1 oz butter
1 onion, peeled and finely chopped
200 g/7 oz Arborio rice
finely grated rind and juice of 1 lemon

50 g/2 oz Parmesan cheese, grated
salt and freshly ground black pepper
freshly grated Parmesan cheese, to serve

Cook the beans in a saucepan of lightly salted boiling water for 4–5 minutes, or until just tender. Drain and plunge into cold water. Peel off the tough outer skins, if liked. Pat the artichokes dry on absorbent kitchen paper and cut each in half lengthways through the stem end. Cut each half into three wedges.

Heat the oil in a large saucepan and cook the artichokes for 4–5 minutes, turning occasionally, until they are lightly browned. Remove and reserve. Bring the wine and stock to the boil in a separate frying pan. Keep them barely simmering while making the risotto.

Melt the butter in a large frying pan, add the onion and cook for 5 minutes until beginning to soften. Add the rice and cook for 1 minute, stirring. Pour in a ladleful of the hot wine and stock, simmer gently, stirring frequently, until the stock is absorbed. Continue to add the stock in this way for 20–25 minutes, until the rice is just tender; the risotto should look creamy and soft.

Add the broad beans, artichokes, and lemon rind and juice. Gently mix in, cover and leave to warm through for 1–2 minutes. Stir in the Parmesan cheese and season to taste with salt and pepper. Serve sprinkled with extra Parmesan cheese.

Try this: FOR AN ALTERNATIVE: 174 FOR ENTERTAINING: 248

Warm Potato, Pear & Pecan Salad

SERVES 4

900 g/2 lb new potatoes,
preferably red-skinned,
unpeeled
salt and freshly ground
black pepper

1 tsp Dijon mustard
2 tsp white wine vinegar
3 tbsp groundnut oil
1 tbsp hazelnut or walnut oil
2 tsp poppy seeds

2 firm ripe dessert pears
2 tsp lemon juice
175 g/6 oz baby
spinach leaves
75 g/3 oz toasted pecan nuts

Scrub the potatoes, then cook in a saucepan of lightly salted boiling water for 15 minutes, or until tender. Drain, cut into halves, or quarters if large, and place in a serving bowl.

In a small bowl or jug, whisk together the mustard and vinegar. Gradually add the oils until the mixture begins to thicken. Stir in the poppy seeds and season to taste with salt and pepper.

Pour about two thirds of the dressing over the hot potatoes and toss gently to coat. Leave until the potatoes have soaked up the dressing and are just warm.

Meanwhile, quarter and core the pears. Cut into thin slices, then sprinkle with the lemon juice to prevent them from going brown. Add to the potatoes with the spinach leaves and toasted pecan nuts. Gently mix together.

Drizzle the remaining dressing over the salad. Serve immediately before the spinach starts to wilt.

Try this: FOR AN ALTERNATIVE: 180   FOR ENTERTAINING: 202

Fusilli Pasta with Spicy Tomato Salsa

SERVES 4

6 large ripe tomatoes
2 tbsp lemon juice
2 tbsp lime juice
grated rind of 1 lime
2 shallots, peeled and

finely chopped
2 garlic cloves, peeled
  and finely chopped
1–2 red chillies
1–2 green chillies

450 g/1 lb fresh fusilli pasta
4 tbsp crème fraîche
2 tbsp freshly chopped basil
sprig of oregano, to garnish

Place the tomatoes in a bowl and cover with boiling water. Allow to stand until the skins start to peel away.

Remove the skins from the tomatoes, divide each tomato in four and remove all the seeds. Chop the flesh into small dice and put in a small pan. Add the lemon and lime juice and the grated lime rind and stir well.

Add the chopped shallots and garlic. Remove the seeds carefully from the chillies, chop finely and add to the pan.

Bring to the boil and simmer gently for 5–10 minutes until the salsa has thickened slightly. Reserve the salsa to allow the flavours to develop while the pasta is cooking.

Bring a large pan of water to the boil and add the pasta. Simmer gently for 3–4 minutes or until the pasta is just tender.

Drain the pasta and rinse in boiling water. Top with a large spoonful of salsa and a small spoonful of crème fraîche. Garnish with the chopped basil and oregano and serve immediately.

Try this: FOR AN ALTERNATIVE: 292   FOR ENTERTAINING: 264

Pasta with Courgettes, Rosemary & Lemon

SERVES 4

350 g/12 oz dried pasta
shapes, e.g. rigatoni
1½ tbsp good quality
extra virgin olive oil
2 garlic cloves, peeled
and finely chopped
4 medium courgettes,
thinly sliced

1 tbsp freshly
chopped rosemary
1 tbsp freshly
chopped parsley
zest and juice of 2 lemons
25 g/1 oz pitted black olives,
roughly chopped
25 g/1 oz pitted green olives,

roughly chopped
salt and freshly ground
black pepper

To garnish:
lemon slices
sprigs of fresh rosemary

Bring a large saucepan of salted water to the boil and add the pasta. Return to the boil and cook until 'al dente', or according to the packet instructions.

Meanwhile, when the pasta is almost done, heat the oil in a large frying pan and add the garlic. Cook over a medium heat until the garlic just begins to brown. Be careful not to overcook the garlic at this stage or it will become bitter.

Add the courgettes, rosemary, parsley and lemon zest and juice. Cook for 3–4 minutes until the courgettes are just tender.

Add the olives to the frying pan and stir well. Season to taste with salt and pepper and remove from the heat.

Drain the pasta well and add to the frying pan. Stir until thoroughly combined. Garnish with lemon and sprigs of fresh rosemary and serve immediately.

Try this: FOR AN ALTERNATIVE: 278   FOR ENTERTAINING: 268

Vegetarian Spaghetti Bolognese

SERVES 4

2 tbsp olive oil
1 onion, peeled and
　finely chopped
1 carrot, peeled and
　finely chopped
1 celery stick, trimmed and
　finely chopped

225 g/8 oz Quorn mince
150 ml/5 fl oz red wine
300 ml/½ pint vegetable
　stock
1 tsp mushroom ketchup
4 tbsp tomato purée
350 g/12 oz dried spaghetti

4 tbsp crème fraîche
salt and freshly ground
　black pepper
1 tbsp freshly
　chopped parsley

Heat the oil in a large saucepan and add the onion, carrot and celery. Cook gently for 10 minutes, adding a little water if necessary, until softened and starting to brown.

Add the Quorn mince and cook a further 2–3 minutes before adding the red wine. Increase the heat and simmer gently until nearly all the wine has evaporated.

Mix together the vegetable stock and mushroom ketchup and add about half to the Quorn mixture along with the tomato purée. Cover and simmer gently for about 45 minutes, adding the remaining stock as necessary.

Meanwhile, bring a large pan of salted water to the boil and add the spaghetti. Cook until 'al dente', or according to the packet instructions. Drain well. Remove the sauce from the heat, add the crème fraîche and season to taste with salt and pepper. Stir in the parsley and serve immediately with the pasta.

 Try this: FOR AN ALTERNATIVE: 320　FOR ENTERTAINING: 226

Tagliatelle with Broccoli & Sesame

SERVES 2

225 g/8 oz broccoli,
cut into florets
125 g/4 oz baby corn
175 g/6 oz dried tagliatelle
1½ tbsp tahini paste
1 tbsp dark soy sauce
1 tbsp dark muscovado sugar

1 tbsp red wine vinegar
1 tbsp sunflower oil
1 garlic clove, peeled
and finely chopped
2.5 cm/1 inch piece fresh
root ginger, peeled
and shredded

½ tsp dried chilli flakes
salt and freshly ground
black pepper
1 tbsp toasted sesame seeds
slices of radish, to garnish

Bring a large saucepan of salted water to the boil and add the broccoli and corn. Return the water to the boil then remove the vegetables at once using a slotted spoon, reserving the water. Plunge them into cold water and drain well. Dry on kitchen paper and reserve.

Return the water to the boil. Add the tagliatelle and cook until 'al dente', or according to the packet instructions. Drain well. Run under cold water until cold, then drain well again.

Place the tahini, soy sauce, sugar and vinegar into a bowl. Mix well, then reserve. Heat the oil in a wok or large frying pan over a high heat and add the garlic, ginger and chilli flakes and stir-fry for about 30 seconds. Add the broccoli and baby corn and continue to stir-fry for about 3 minutes.

Add the tagliatelle to the wok along with the tahini mixture and stir together for a further 1–2 minutes until heated through. Season to taste with salt and pepper. Sprinkle with sesame seeds, garnish with the radish slices and serve immediately.

Try this: FOR AN ALTERNATIVE: 300   FOR ENTERTAINING: 298

Rice & Vegetable Timbale

SERVES 6

25 g/1 oz dried white
  breadcrumbs
3 tbsp olive oil
2 courgettes, sliced
1 small aubergine, cut into
  1 cm/½ inch dice
175 g/6 oz mushrooms,
  sliced
1 garlic clove, peeled
  and crushed

1 tsp balsamic vinegar
1 onion, peeled and
  finely chopped
25 g/1 oz unsalted butter
400 g/14 oz Arborio rice
about 1.3 litres/2¼ pints
  boiling vegetable stock
2 medium eggs,
  lightly beaten
25 g/1 oz Parmesan cheese,

  finely grated
2 tbsp freshly chopped basil
salt and freshly ground
  black pepper

To garnish:
sprig of fresh basil
1 radish, thinly sliced

Preheat the oven to 190°C/375°F/Gas Mark 5, 10 minutes before cooking. Sprinkle the breadcrumbs over the base and sides of a thickly buttered 20.5 cm/8 inch round loose-bottomed tin. Heat the olive oil in a large frying pan and gently fry the courgettes, aubergine, mushrooms and garlic for 5 minutes, or until beginning to soften. Stir in the vinegar. Tip the vegetables into a large sieve placed over a bowl to catch the juices. Fry the onion gently in the butter for 10 minutes, until soft. Add the rice and stir for a minute to coat. Add a ladleful of stock and any juices from the vegetables and simmer, stirring, until the rice has absorbed all of the liquid. Continue adding the stock in this way until the rice is just tender. This should take about 20 minutes. Remove from the heat and leave to cool for 5 minutes. Stir in the eggs, cheese and basil. Season to taste with salt and pepper.

Spoon a quarter of the rice into the prepared tin. Top with one third of the vegetable mixture. Continue layering up in this way, finishing with a layer of rice. Level the top of the layer of rice, gently pressing down the mixture. Cover with a piece of tinfoil. Put on a baking sheet and bake in the preheated oven for 50 minutes, or until firm. Leave the timbale to stand in the tin for 10 minutes, still covered with tinfoil, then turn out on to a warmed serving platter. Garnish with a sprig of fresh basil and slices of radish and serve immediately.

Vegetables Braised in Olive Oil & Lemon

SERVES 4

small strip of pared rind and
   juice of ½ lemon
4 tbsp olive oil
1 bay leaf
large sprig of thyme
150 ml/¼ pint water
4 spring onions, trimmed

and finely chopped
175 g/6 oz baby button
   mushrooms
175 g/6 oz broccoli, cut into
   small florets
175 g/6 oz cauliflower, cut
   into small florets

1 medium courgette, sliced
   on the diagonal
2 tbsp freshly snipped
   chives
salt and freshly ground
   black pepper
lemon zest, to garnish

Put the pared lemon rind and juice into a large saucepan. Add the olive oil, bay leaf, thyme and the water. Bring to the boil. Add the spring onions and mushrooms. Top with the broccoli and cauliflower, trying to add them so that the stalks are submerged in the water and the tops are just above it. Cover and simmer for 3 minutes.

Scatter the courgettes on top, so that they are steamed rather than boiled. Cook, covered, for a further 3–4 minutes, until all the vegetables are tender. Using a slotted spoon, transfer the vegetables from the liquid into a warmed serving dish. Increase the heat and boil rapidly for 3–4 minutes, or until the liquid is reduced to about 8 tablespoons. Remove the lemon rind, bay leaf and thyme sprig and discard.

Stir the chives into the reduced liquid, season to taste with salt and pepper and pour over the vegetables. Sprinkle with lemon zest and serve immediately.

Try this: FOR AN ALTERNATIVE: 246 FOR ENTERTAINING: 342

Melanzane Parmigiana

SERVES 4

900 g/2 lb aubergines
salt and freshly ground
 black pepper
5 tbsp olive oil
1 red onion, peeled
 and chopped
½ tsp mild paprika pepper

150 ml/¼ pint dry red wine
150 ml/¼ pint vegetable
 stock
400 g can chopped tomatoes
1 tsp tomato purée
1 tbsp freshly chopped
 oregano

175 g/6 oz mozzarella
 cheese, thinly sliced
40 g/1½ oz Parmesan
 cheese, coarsely grated
sprig of fresh basil, to
 garnish

Preheat the oven to 200°C/400°F/Gas Mark 6, 15 minutes before cooking. Cut the aubergines lengthways into thin slices. Sprinkle with salt and leave to drain in a colander over a bowl for 30 minutes.

Meanwhile, heat 1 tablespoon of the olive oil in a saucepan and fry the onion for 10 minutes, until softened. Add the paprika and cook for 1 minute. Stir in the wine, stock, tomatoes and tomato purée. Simmer, uncovered, for 25 minutes, or until fairly thick. Stir in the oregano and season to taste with salt and pepper. Remove from the heat.

Rinse the aubergine slices thoroughly under cold water and pat dry on absorbent kitchen paper. Heat 2 tablespoons of the oil in a griddle pan and cook the aubergines in batches, for 3 minutes on each side, until golden. Drain well on absorbent kitchen paper.

Pour half of the tomato sauce into the base of a large ovenproof dish. Cover with half the aubergine slices, then top with the mozzarella. Cover with the remaining aubergine slices and pour over the remaining tomato sauce. Sprinkle with the grated Parmesan cheese.

Bake in the preheated oven for 30 minutes, or until the aubergines are tender and the sauce is bubbling. Garnish with a sprig of fresh basil and cool for a few minutes before serving.

Try this: FOR AN ALTERNATIVE: 282 FOR ENTERTAINING: 318

Stuffed Tomatoes with Grilled Polenta

SERVES 4

For the polenta:
300 ml/½ pint vegetable
    stock
salt and freshly ground
    black pepper
50 g/2 oz quick-cook polenta
15 g/½ oz butter

For the stuffed tomotoes:
4 large tomatoes
1 tbsp olive oil
1 garlic clove, peeled
    and crushed
1 bunch spring onions,
    trimmed and finely
    chopped

2 tbsp freshly
    chopped parsley
2 tbsp freshly chopped basil
50 g/2 oz fresh white
    breadcrumbs
snipped chives, to garnish

Preheat the grill just before cooking. To make the polenta, pour the stock into a saucepan. Add a pinch of salt and bring to the boil. Pour in the polenta in a fine stream, stirring all the time. Simmer for about 15 minutes, or until very thick. Stir in the butter and add a little pepper. Turn the polenta out on to a chopping board and spread to a thickness of just over 1 cm/½ inch. Cool, cover with clingfilm and chill in the refrigerator for 30 minutes.

To make the stuffed tomatoes, cut the tomatoes in half then scoop out the seeds and press through a fine sieve to extract the juices. Season the insides of the tomatoes with salt and pepper and reserve. Heat the olive oil in a saucepan and gently fry the garlic and spring onions for 3 minutes. Add the tomatoes' juices, bubble for 3–4 minutes, until most of the liquid has evaporated. Stir in the herbs and a little black pepper with half the breadcrumbs. Spoon into the hollowed out tomatoes and reserve.

Cut the polenta into 5 cm/2 inch squares, then cut each in half diagonally to make triangles. Put the triangles on a piece of tinfoil on the grill rack and grill for 4–5 minutes on each side, until golden. Cover and keep warm. Grill the tomatoes under a medium-hot grill for about 4 minutes. Sprinkle with the remaining breadcrumbs and grill for 1–2 minutes, or until golden brown. Garnish with snipped chives and serve immediately with the grilled polenta.

Rice–filled Peppers

SERVES 4

8 ripe tomatoes
2 tbsp olive oil
1 onion, peeled and
   chopped
1 garlic clove, peeled
   and crushed
½ tsp dark muscovado sugar

125 g/4 oz cooked
   long-grain rice
50 g/2 oz pine nuts, toasted
1 tbsp freshly chopped
   oregano
salt and freshly ground
   black pepper

2 large red peppers
2 large yellow peppers

To serve:
mixed salad
crusty bread

Preheat the oven to 200°C/400°F/Gas Mark 6. Put the tomatoes in a small bowl and pour over boiling water to cover. Leave for 1 minute, then drain. Plunge the tomatoes into cold water to cool, then peel off the skins. Quarter, remove the seeds and chop.

Heat the olive oil in a frying pan, and cook the onion gently for 10 minutes, until softened. Add the garlic, chopped tomatoes and sugar. Gently cook the tomato mixture for 10 minutes until thickened. Remove from the heat and stir the rice, pine nuts and oregano into the sauce. Season to taste with salt and pepper.

Halve the peppers lengthways, cutting through and leaving the stem on. Remove the seeds and cores, then put the peppers in a lightly oiled roasting tin, cut-side down and cook in the preheated oven for about 10 minutes.

Turn the peppers so they are cut-side up. Spoon in the filling, then cover with tinfoil. Return to the oven for 15 minutes, or until the peppers are very tender, removing the tinfoil for the last 5 minutes to allow the tops to brown a little. Serve one red pepper half and one yellow pepper half per person with a mixed salad and plenty of warmed, crusty bread.

Try this: FOR AN ALTERNATIVE: 214   FOR ENTERTAINING: 212

Roasted Red Pepper, Tomato & Red Onion Soup

SERVES 4

fine spray of oil
2 large red peppers, deseeded and roughly chopped
1 red onion, peeled and roughly chopped

350 g/12 oz tomatoes, halved
1 small crusty French loaf
1 garlic clove, peeled
600 ml/1 pint vegetable stock

salt and freshly ground black pepper
1 tsp Worcestershire sauce
4 tbsp fromage frais

Preheat the oven to 190°C/375°F/Gas Mark 5. Spray a large roasting tin with the oil and place the peppers and onion in the base. Cook in the oven for 10 minutes. Add the tomatoes and cook for a further 20 minutes or until the peppers are soft.

Cut the bread into 1 cm/½ inch slices. Cut the garlic clove in half and rub the cut edge of the garlic over the bread. Place all the bread slices on a large baking tray, and bake in the preheated oven for 10 minutes, turning halfway through, until golden and crisp.

Remove the vegetables from the oven and allow to cool slightly, then blend in a food processor until smooth. Strain the vegetable mixture through a large nylon sieve into a saucepan, to remove the seeds and skin. Add the stock, season to taste with salt and pepper and stir to mix. Heat the soup gently until piping hot.

In a small bowl beat together the Worcestershire sauce with the fromage frais. Pour the soup into warmed bowls and swirl a spoonful of the fromage frais mixture into each bowl. Serve immediately with the garlic toasts.

Try this: FOR AN ALTERNATIVE: 170 FOR ENTERTAINING: 210

Rigatoni with Oven–dried Cherry Tomatoes & Mascarpone

SERVES 4

350 g/12 oz red cherry
   tomatoes
1 tsp caster sugar
salt and freshly ground
   black pepper

2 tbsp olive oil
400 g/14 oz dried rigatoni
125 g/4 oz petits pois
2 tbsp mascarpone cheese
1 tbsp freshly chopped mint

1 tbsp freshly
   chopped parsley
sprigs of fresh mint,
   to garnish

Preheat the oven to 140°C/275°F/Gas Mark 1. Halve the cherry tomatoes and place close together on a non-stick baking tray, cut-side up. Sprinkle lightly with the sugar, then with a little salt and pepper.

Bake in the preheated oven for 1¼ hours, or until dry, but not beginning to colour. Leave to cool on the baking tray. Put in a bowl, drizzle over the olive oil and toss to coat.

Bring a large saucepan of lightly salted water to the boil and cook the pasta for about 10 minutes or until 'al dente'. Add the petits pois, 2–3 minutes before the end of the cooking time. Drain thoroughly and return the pasta and the petits pois to the saucepan.

Add the mascarpone to the saucepan. When melted, add the tomatoes, mint, parsley and a little black pepper. Toss gently together, then transfer to a warmed serving dish or individual plates and garnish with sprigs of fresh mint. Serve immediately.

Try this: FOR AN ALTERNATIVE: 106   FOR ENTERTAINING: 224

Spinach Dumplings with Rich Tomato Sauce

SERVES 4

For the sauce:
2 tbsp olive oil
1 onion, peeled and chopped
1 garlic clove,
   peeled and crushed
1 red chilli, deseeded
   and chopped
150 ml/¼ pint dry white wine
400 g can chopped tomatoes
pared strip of lemon rind

For the dumplings:
450 g/1 lb fresh spinach
50 g/2 oz ricotta cheese
25 g/1 oz fresh white
   breadcrumbs
25 g/1 oz Parmesan
   cheese, grated
1 medium egg yolk
¼ tsp freshly grated nutmeg
salt and freshly ground

   black pepper
5 tbsp plain flour
2 tbsp olive oil, for frying
fresh basil leaves, to garnish
freshly cooked tagliatelle,
   to serve

To make the tomato sauce, heat the olive oil in a large saucepan and fry the onion gently for 5 minutes. Add the garlic and chilli and cook for a further 5 minutes, until softened.

Stir in the wine, chopped tomatoes and lemon rind. Bring to the boil, cover and simmer for 20 minutes, then uncover and simmer for 15 minutes, or until the sauce has thickened. Remove the lemon rind and season to taste with salt and pepper.

To make the spinach dumplings, wash the spinach thoroughly and remove any tough stalks. Cover and cook in a large saucepan over a low heat with just the water clinging to the leaves. Drain, then squeeze out all the excess water. Finely chop and put in a large bowl. Add the ricotta, breadcrumbs, Parmesan cheeseand egg yolk to the spinach. Season with nutmeg and salt and pepper. Mix together and shape into 20 walnut-sized balls.

Toss the spinach balls in the flour. Heat the olive oil in a large, non-stick frying pan and fry the balls gently for 5–6 minutes, carefully turning occasionally. Garnish with fresh basil leaves and serve immediately with the tomato sauce and tagliatelle.

Try this: FOR AN ALTERNATIVE: 64   FOR ENTERTAINING: 228

Aubergine Cannelloni with Watercress Sauce

SERVES 4

4 large aubergines, about
   250 g/9 oz each
5–6 tbsp olive oil
350 g/12 oz ricotta cheese
75 g/3 oz Parmesan
   cheese, grated
3 tbsp freshly chopped basil
salt and freshly ground

black pepper

For the watercress sauce:
75 g/3 oz watercress,
   trimmed
200 ml/⅓ pint
   vegetable stock
1 shallot, peeled and sliced

pared strip of lemon rind
1 large sprig of thyme
3 tbsp crème fraîche
1 tsp lemon juice

To garnish:
sprigs of watercress
lemon zest

Preheat the oven to 190°C/375°F/Gas Mark 5, 10 minutes before cooking. Cut the aubergines lengthways into thin slices, discarding the side pieces. Heat 2 tablespoons of oil in a frying pan and cook the aubergine slices in a single layer in several batches, turning once, until golden on both sides.

Mix the cheeses, basil and seasoning together. Lay the aubergine slices on a clean surface and spread the cheese mixture evenly between them. Roll up the slices from one of the short ends to enclose the filling. Place, seam-side down in a single layer in an ovenproof dish. Bake in the preheated oven for 15 minutes, or until golden.

To make the watercress sauce, blanch the watercress leaves in boiling water for about 30 seconds. Drain well, then rinse in a sieve under cold running water and squeeze dry. Put the stock, shallot, lemon rind and thyme in a small saucepan. Boil rapidly until reduced by half, then remove from the heat and strain. Put the watercress and strained stock in a food processor and blend until fairly smooth. Return to the saucepan, stir in the crème fraîche, lemon juice and season to taste with salt and pepper. Heat gently until the sauce is piping hot. Serve a little of the sauce drizzled over the aubergines and the rest separately in a jug. Garnish the cannelloni with sprigs of watercress and lemon zest. Serve immediately.

Panzanella

SERVES 4

250 g/9 oz day-old Italian-style bread
1 tbsp red wine vinegar
4 tbsp olive oil
1 tsp lemon juice
1 small garlic clove, peeled and finely chopped

1 red onion, peeled and finely sliced
1 cucumber, peeled if preferred
225 g/8 oz ripe tomatoes, deseeded
150 g/5 oz pitted black olives

about 20 basil leaves, coarsely torn or left whole if small
sea salt and freshly ground black pepper

Cut the bread into thick slices, leaving the crusts on. Add 1 teaspoon of red wine vinegar to a jug of iced water, put the slices of bread in a bowl and pour over the water. Make sure the bread is covered completely. Leave to soak for 3–4 minutes until just soft.

Remove the soaked bread from the water and squeeze it gently, first with your hands and then in a clean tea towel to remove any excess water. Put the bread on a plate, cover with clingfilm and chill in the refrigerator for about 1 hour.

Meanwhile, whisk together the olive oil, the remaining red wine vinegar and lemon juice in a large serving bowl. Add the garlic and onion and stir to coat well.

Halve the cucumber and remove the seeds. Chop both the cucumber and tomatoes into 1 cm/½ inch dice. Add to the garlic and onions with the olives. Tear the bread into bite-sized chunks and add to the bowl with the fresh basil leaves. Toss together to mix and serve immediately, with a grinding of sea salt and black pepper.

Try this: FOR AN ALTERNATIVE: 216   FOR ENTERTAINING: 256

Vegetable Frittata

SERVES 2

6 medium eggs
2 tbsp freshly
   chopped parsley
1 tbsp freshly
   chopped tarragon
25 g/1 oz pecorino or
   Parmesan cheese,
   finely grated

freshly ground black pepper
175 g/6 oz tiny new potatoes
2 small carrots, peeled
   and sliced
125 g/4 oz broccoli, cut
   into small florets
1 courgette, about 125 g/
   4 oz, sliced

2 tbsp olive oil
4 spring onions, trimmed
   and thinly sliced

To serve:
   mixed green salad
   crusty Italian bread

Preheat the grill just before cooking. Lightly beat the eggs with the parsley, tarragon and half the cheese. Season to taste with black pepper and reserve. (Salt is not needed as the pecorino is very salty.)

Bring a large saucepan of lightly salted water to the boil. Add the new potatoes and cook for 8 minutes. Add the carrots and cook for 4 minutes, then add the broccoli florets and the courgettes and cook for a further 3–4 minutes, or until all the vegetables are barely tender. Drain well. Heat the oil in a 20.5 cm/8 inch heavy-based frying pan. Add the spring onions and cook for 3–4 minutes, or until softened. Add all the vegetables and cook for a few seconds, then pour in the beaten egg mixture.

Stir gently for about a minute, then cook for a further 1–2 minutes, or until the bottom of the frittata is set and golden brown. Place the pan under a hot grill for 1 minute, or until almost set and just beginning to brown. Sprinkle with the remaining cheese and grill for a further 1 minute, or until it is lightly browned.

Loosen the edges and slide out of the pan. Cut into wedges and serve hot or warm with a mixed green salad and crusty Italian bread.

Try this: FOR AN ALTERNATIVE: 82 FOR ENTERTAINING: 166

Panzerotti

SERVES 16

450 g/1 lb strong white flour
pinch of salt
1 tsp easy-blend dried yeast
2 tbsp olive oil
300 ml/½ pint warm water
fresh rocket leaves, to serve

For the filling:
1 tbsp olive oil

1 small red onion, peeled
   and finely chopped
2 garlic cloves, peeled and
   crushed
½ yellow pepper, deseeded
   and chopped
1 small courgette, about 75 g/
   3 oz, trimmed and
   chopped

50 g/2 oz black olives, pitted
   and quartered
125 g/4 oz mozzarella
   cheese, cut into tiny cubes
salt and freshly ground
   black pepper
5–6 tbsp tomato purée
1 tsp dried mixed herbs
oil for deep-frying

Sift the flour and salt into a bowl. Stir in the yeast. Make a well in the centre. Add the oil and the warm water and mix to a soft dough. Knead on a lightly floured surface until smooth and elastic. Put in an oiled bowl, cover and leave in a warm place to rise while making the filling.

To make the filling, heat the oil in a frying pan and cook the onion for 5 minutes. Add the garlic, yellow pepper and courgette. Cook for about 5 minutes, or until the vegetables are tender. Tip into a bowl and leave to cool slightly. Stir in the olives, mozzarella cheese and season to taste with salt and pepper. Briefly re-knead the dough. Divide into 16 equal pieces. Roll out each to a circle about 10 cm/4 inches. Mix together the tomato purée and dried herbs, then spread about 1 teaspoon on each circle, leaving a 2 cm/¾ inch border around the edge. Divide the filling equally between the circles, it will seem a small amount, but if you overfill, they will leak during cooking. Brush the edges with water, then fold in half to enclose the filling. Press to seal, then crimp the edges.

Heat the oil in a deep-fat fryer to 180°C/350°F. Deep-fry the panzerotti in batches for 3 minutes, or until golden. Drain on absorbent kitchen paper and keep warm in a low oven until ready to serve with fresh rocket.

Try this: FOR AN ALTERNATIVE: 334   FOR ENTERTAINING: 344

Pasta Primavera

SERVES 4

150 g/5 oz French beans
150 g/5 oz sugar snap peas
40 g/1½ oz butter
1 tsp olive oil
225 g/8 oz baby carrots,
    scrubbed
2 courgettes, trimmed and
    thinly sliced

175 g/6 oz baby leeks,
    trimmed and cut into
    2.5 cm/1 inch lengths
200 ml/7 fl oz double cream
1 tsp finely grated
    lemon rind
350 g/12 oz dried tagliatelle
25 g/1 oz Parmesan

cheese, grated
1 tbsp freshly
    snipped chives
1 tbsp freshly chopped dill
salt and freshly ground
    black pepper
sprigs of fresh dill,
    to garnish

Trim and halve the French beans. Bring a large saucepan of lightly salted water to the boil and cook the beans for 4–5 minutes, adding the sugar snap peas after 2 minutes, so that both are tender at the same time. Drain the beans and sugar snap peas and briefly rinse under cold running water.

Heat the butter and oil in a large, non-stick frying pan. Add the baby carrots and cook for 2 minutes, then stir in the courgettes and leeks and cook for 10 minutes, stirring, until the vegetables are almost tender. Stir the cream and lemon rind into the vegetables and bubble over a gentle heat until the sauce is slightly reduced and the vegetables are cooked.

Meanwhile, bring a large saucepan of lightly salted water to the boil and cook the tagliatelle for 10 minutes, or until 'al dente'.

Add the beans, sugar snaps, Parmesan cheese and herbs to the sauce. Stir for 30 seconds, or until the cheese has melted and the vegetables are hot. Drain the tagliatelle, add the vegetables and sauce, then toss gently to mix and season to taste with salt and pepper. Spoon into a warmed serving bowl and garnish with a few sprigs of dill and serve immediately.

 Try this: FOR AN ALTERNATIVE: 260   FOR ENTERTAINING: 278

Pasta Shells with Broccoli & Capers

SERVES 4

400 g/14 oz conchiglie (pasta shells)
450 g/1 lb broccoli florets, cut into small pieces
5 tbsp olive oil
1 large onion, peeled and finely chopped

4 tbsp capers in brine, rinsed and drained
½ tsp dried chilli flakes (optional)
75 g/3 oz freshly grated Parmesan cheese, plus extra

to serve
25 g/1 oz pecorino cheese, grated
salt and freshly ground black pepper
2 tbsp freshly chopped flat leaf parsley, to garnish

Bring a large pan of lightly salted water to a rolling boil. Add the pasta, return to the boil and cook for 2 minutes. Add the broccoli to the pan. Return to the boil and continue cooking for 8–10 minutes, or until the conchiglie is 'al dente'.

Meanwhile, heat the olive oil in a large frying pan, add the onion and cook for 5 minutes, or until softened, stirring frequently. Stir in the capers and chilli flakes, if using, and cook for a further 2 minutes.

Drain the pasta and broccoli and add to the frying pan. Toss the ingredients to mix thoroughly. Sprinkle over the cheeses, then stir until the cheeses have just melted. Season to taste with salt and pepper, then tip into a warmed serving dish. Garnish with chopped parsley and serve immediately with extra Parmesan cheese.

Try this: FOR AN ALTERNATIVE: 264   FOR ENTERTAINING: 260

Italian Baked Tomatoes with Curly Endive & Radicchio

SERVES 4

1 tsp olive oil
4 beef tomatoes
salt
50 g/2 oz fresh white
   breadcrumbs
1 tbsp freshly
   snipped chives
1 tbsp freshly

chopped parsley
125 g/4 oz button
   mushrooms,
   finely chopped
salt and freshly ground
   black pepper
25 g/1 oz fresh Parmesan
   cheese, grated

For the salad:
½ curly endive lettuce
½ small piece of radicchio
2 tbsp olive oil
1 tsp balsamic vinegar
salt and freshly ground
   black pepper

Preheat oven to 190°C/375°F/Gas Mark 5. Lightly oil a baking tray with the teaspoon of oil. Slice the tops off the tomatoes and remove all the tomato flesh and sieve into a large bowl. Sprinkle a little salt inside the tomato shells and then place them upside down on a plate while the filling is prepared.

Mix the sieved tomato with the breadcrumbs, fresh herbs and mushrooms and season well with salt and pepper. Place the tomato shells on the prepared baking tray and fill with the tomato and mushroom mixture. Sprinkle the cheese on the top and bake in the preheated oven for 15–20 minutes, until golden brown.

Meanwhile, prepare the salad. Arrange the endive and radicchio on individual serving plates and mix the remaining ingredients together in a small bowl to make the dressing. Season to taste.

When the tomatoes are cooked, allow to rest for 5 minutes, then place on the prepared plates and drizzle over a little dressing. Serve warm.

Try this: FOR AN ALTERNATIVE: 296   FOR ENTERTAINING: 214

Pastini–stuffed Peppers

SERVES 6

6 red, yellow or orange
   peppers, tops cut off
   and deseeded
salt and freshly ground
   black pepper
175 g/6 oz pastini
4 tbsp olive oil
1 onion, peeled and
   finely chopped
2 garlic cloves, peeled and

finely chopped
3 ripe plum tomatoes,
   skinned, deseeded
   and chopped
50 ml/2 fl oz dry white wine
8 pitted black olives,
   chopped
4 tbsp freshly chopped
   mixed herbs, such as
   parsley, basil, oregano or

marjoram
125 g/4 oz mozzarella
   cheese, diced
4 tbsp grated Parmesan
   cheese
fresh tomato sauce,
   preferably homemade,
   to serve

Preheat the oven to 190°C/375°F/Gas Mark 5, 10 minutes before cooking. Bring a pan of water to the boil. Trim the bottom of each pepper so it sits straight. Blanch the peppers for 2–3 minutes, then drain on absorbent kitchen paper. Return the water to the boil, add ½ teaspoon of salt and the pastini and cook for 3–4 minutes, or until 'al dente'. Drain thoroughly, reserving the water. Rinse under cold running water, drain again and reserve.

Heat 2 tablespoons of the olive oil in a large frying pan, add the onion and cook for 3–4 minutes. Add the garlic and cook for 1 minute. Stir in the tomatoes and wine and cook for 5 minutes, stirring frequently. Add the olives, herbs, mozzarella cheese and half the Parmesan cheese. Season to taste with salt and pepper. Remove from the heat and stir in the pastini.

Dry the insides of the peppers with absorbent kitchen paper, then season lightly. Arrange the peppers in a lightly oiled shallow baking dish and fill with the pastini mixture. Sprinkle with the remaining Parmesan cheese and drizzle over the remaining oil. Pour in boiling water to come 1 cm/½ inch up the sides of the dish. Cook in the preheated oven for 25 minutes, or until cooked. Serve immediately with freshly made tomato sauce.

Try this: FOR AN ALTERNATIVE: 212   FOR ENTERTAINING: 272

Fusilli with Courgettes & Sun–dried Tomatoes

SERVES 6

5 tbsp olive oil
1 large onion, peeled and
   thinly sliced
2 garlic cloves, peeled and
   finely chopped
700 g/1½ lb courgettes,
   trimmed and sliced

400 g can chopped
   plum tomatoes
12 sun-dried tomatoes, cut
   into thin strips
salt and freshly ground
   black pepper
450 g/1 lb fusilli

25 g/1 oz butter, diced
2 tbsp freshly chopped basil
   or flat leaf parsley
grated Parmesan or
   pecorino cheese,
   for serving

Heat 2 tablespoons of the olive oil in a large frying pan, add the onion and cook for 5-7 minutes, or until softened. Add the chopped garlic and courgette slices and cook for a further 5 minutes, stirring occasionally.

Stir the chopped tomatoes and the sun-dried tomatoes into the frying pan and season to taste with salt and pepper. Cook until the courgettes are just tender and the sauce is slightly thickened.

Bring a large pan of lightly salted water to a rolling boil. Add the fusilli and cook according to the packet instructions, or until 'al dente'.

Drain the fusilli thoroughly and return to the pan. Add the butter and remaining oil and toss to coat. Stir the chopped basil or parsley into the courgette mixture and pour over the fusilli. Toss and tip into a warmed serving dish. Serve with grated Parmesan or pecorino cheese.

Try this: FOR AN ALTERNATIVE: 306   FOR ENTERTAINING: 338

Tagliatelle Primavera

SERVES 4

125 g/4 oz asparagus, lightly peeled and cut into 6.5 cm/2½ inch lengths
125 g/4 oz carrots, peeled and cut into julienne strips
125 g/4 oz courgettes, trimmed and cut into julienne strips
50 g/2 oz small mangetout

50 g/2 oz butter
1 small onion, peeled and finely chopped
1 small red pepper, deseeded and finely chopped
50 ml/2 fl oz dry vermouth
225 ml/8 fl oz double cream
1 small leek, trimmed and cut into julienne strips

75 g/3 oz fresh green peas (or frozen, thawed)
salt and freshly ground black pepper
400 g/14 oz fresh tagliatelle
2 tbsp freshly chopped flat leaf parsley
25 g/1 oz Parmesan cheese, grated

Bring a medium saucepan of salted water to the boil. Add the asparagus and blanch for 1–2 minutes, or until just beginning to soften. Using a slotted spoon, transfer to a colander and rinse under cold running water. Repeat with the carrots and courgettes. Add the mangetout, return to the boil, drain, rinse immediately and drain again. Reserve the blanched vegetables.

Heat the butter in a large frying pan, add the onion and red pepper and cook for 5 minutes, or until they begin to soften and colour. Pour in the dry vermouth; it will bubble and steam and evaporate almost immediately. Stir in the cream and simmer over a medium-low heat until reduced by about half. Add the blanched vegetables with the leeks, peas and seasoning and heat through for 2 minutes.

Meanwhile, bring a large saucepan of lightly salted water to the boil, add the tagliatelle and return to the boil. Cook for 2-3 minutes, or until 'al dente'. Drain thoroughly and return to the pan. Stir the chopped parsley into the cream and vegetable sauce then pour over the pasta and toss to coat. Sprinkle with the grated Parmesan cheese and toss lightly. Tip into a warmed serving bowl or spoon on to individual plates and serve immediately.

Try this: FOR AN ALTERNATIVE: 292   FOR ENTERTAINING: 108

Aubergine & Ravioli Parmigiana

SERVES 6

4 tbsp olive oil
1 large onion, peeled and
   finely chopped
2–3 garlic cloves, peeled
   and crushed
2 x 400 g cans chopped
   tomatoes
2 tsp brown sugar
1 dried bay leaf
1 tsp dried oregano

1 tsp dried basil
2 tbsp freshly shredded basil
salt and freshly ground
   black pepper
2–3 medium aubergines,
   sliced crosswwise 1 cm/
   ½ inch thick
2 medium eggs, beaten
   with 1 tbsp water
125 g/4 oz dried

breadcrumbs
75 g/3 oz freshly grated
   Parmesan cheese
400 g/14 oz mozzarella
   cheese, thinly sliced
250 g/9 oz cheese-filled
   ravioli, cooked and
   drained

Preheat the oven to 180°C/350°F/Gas Mark 4, about 15 minutes before cooking. Heat 2 tablespoons of the olive oil in a large, heavy-based pan, add the onion and cook for 6–7 minutes, or until softened. Add the garlic, cook for 1 minute then stir in the tomatoes, sugar, bay leaf, dried oregano and basil, then bring to the boil, stirring frequently. Simmer for 30–35 minutes, or until thickened and reduced, stirring occasionally. Stir in the fresh basil and season to taste with salt and pepper. Remove the tomato sauce from the heat and reserve.

Heat the remaining olive oil in a large, heavy-based frying pan over a high heat. Dip the aubergine slices in the egg mixture then in the breadcrumbs. Cook in batches until golden on both sides. Drain on absorbent kitchen paper. Add more oil between batches if necessary. Spoon a little tomato sauce into the base of a lightly oiled large baking dish. Cover with a layer of aubergine slices, a sprinkling of Parmesan cheese, a layer of mozzarella cheese, then more sauce. Repeat the layers then cover the sauce with a layer of cooked ravioli. Continue to layer in this way, ending with a layer of mozzarella cheese. Sprinkle the top with Parmesan cheese. Drizzle with a little extra olive oil if liked, then bake in the preheated oven for 30 minutes, or until golden-brown and bubbling. Serve immediately.

    Try this: FOR AN ALTERNATIVE: 318   FOR ENTERTAINING: 306

Mediterranean Rice Salad

SERVES 4

250 g/9 oz Camargue
  red rice
2 sun-dried tomatoes,
  finely chopped
2 garlic cloves, peeled
  and finely chopped
4 tbsp oil from a jar of
  sun-dried tomatoes
2 tsp balsamic vinegar

2 tsp red wine vinegar
salt and freshly ground
  black pepper
1 red onion, peeled and
  thinly sliced
1 yellow pepper, quartered
  and deseeded
1 red pepper, quartered
  and deseeded

½ cucumber,
  peeled and diced
6 ripe plum tomatoes,
  cut into wedges
1 fennel bulb, halved
  and thinly sliced
fresh basil leaves,
  to garnish

Cook the rice in a saucepan of lightly salted boiling water for 35–40 minutes, or until tender. Drain well and reserve.

Whisk the sun-dried tomatoes, garlic, oil and vinegars together in a small bowl or jug. Season to taste with salt and pepper. Put the red onion in a large bowl, pour over the dressing and leave to allow the flavours to develop.

Put the peppers skin-side up on a grill rack and cook under a preheated hot grill for 5–6 minutes, or until blackened and charred. Remove and place in a plastic bag. When cool enough to handle, peel off the skins and slice the peppers.

Add the peppers, cucumber, tomatoes, fennel and rice to the onions. Mix gently together to coat in the dressing. Cover and chill in the refrigerator for 30 minutes to allow the flavours to mingle.

Remove the salad from the refrigerator and leave to stand at room temperature for 20 minutes. Garnish with fresh basil leaves and serve.

 Try this: FOR AN ALTERNATIVE: 182 FOR ENTERTAINING: 114

Courgette Lasagne

SERVES 8

2 tbsp olive oil
1 medium onion, peeled and
    finely chopped
225 g/8 oz mushrooms,
    wiped and thinly sliced
3–4 courgettes, trimmed and
    thinly sliced
2 garlic cloves, peeled and

    finely chopped
½ tsp dried thyme
1–2 tbsp freshly chopped
    basil or flat leaf parsley
salt and freshly ground
    black pepper
1 quantity ready-prepared
    white sauce

350 g/12 oz lasagne
    sheets, cooked
225 g/8 oz mozzarella
    cheese, grated
50 g/2 oz Parmesan
    cheese, grated
400 g can chopped
    tomatoes, drained

Preheat the oven to 200°C/400°F/Gas Mark 6, 15 minutes before cooking. Heat the oil in a large frying pan, add the onion and cook for 3–5 minutes. Add the mushrooms, cook for 2 minutes, then add the courgettes and cook for a further 3–4 minutes, or until tender. Stir in the garlic, thyme and basil or parsley and season to taste with salt and pepper. Remove from the heat and reserve.

Spoon one third of the white sauce on to the base of a lightly oiled large baking dish. Arrange a layer of lasagne over the sauce. Spread half the courgette mixture over the pasta, then sprinkle with some of the mozzarella and some of the Parmesan cheese. Repeat with more white sauce and another layer of lasagne, then cover with half the drained tomatoes.

Cover the tomatoes with lasagne, the remaining courgette mixture, and some mozzarella and Parmesan cheese. Repeat the layers ending with a layer of lasagne sheets, white sauce and the remaining Parmesan cheese. Bake in the preheated oven for 35 minutes, or until golden. Serve immediately.

     Try this: FOR AN ALTERNATIVE: 322   FOR ENTERTAINING: 90

Tortellini & Summer Vegetable Salad

SERVES 6

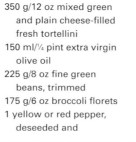

350 g/12 oz mixed green and plain cheese-filled fresh tortellini
150 ml/¼ pint extra virgin olive oil
225 g/8 oz fine green beans, trimmed
175 g/6 oz broccoli florets
1 yellow or red pepper, deseeded and

thinly sliced
1 red onion, peeled and sliced
175 g jar marinated artichoke hearts, drained and halved
2 tbsp capers
75 g/3 oz dry-cured pitted black olives
3 tbsp raspberry or

balsamic vinegar
1 tbsp Dijon mustard
1 tsp soft brown sugar
salt and freshly ground black pepper
2 tbsp freshly chopped basil or flat leaf parsley
2 quartered hard-boiled eggs, to garnish

Bring a large pan of lightly salted water to a rolling boil. Add the tortellini and cook according to the packet instructions, or until 'al dente'.

Using a large slotted spoon, transfer the tortellini to a colander to drain. Rinse under cold running water and drain again. Transfer to a large bowl and toss with 2 tablespoons of the olive oil.

Return the pasta water to the boil and drop in the green beans and broccoli florets; blanch them for 2 minutes, or until just beginning to soften. Drain, rinse under cold running water and drain again thoroughly. Add the vegetables to the reserved tortellini. Add the pepper, onion, artichoke hearts, capers and olives to the bowl; stir lightly.

Whisk together the vinegar, mustard and brown sugar in a bowl and season to taste with salt and pepper. Slowly whisk in the remaining olive oil to form a thick, creamy dressing. Pour over the tortellini and vegetables, add the chopped basil or parsley and stir until lightly coated. Transfer to a shallow serving dish or salad bowl. Garnish with the hard-boiled egg quarters and serve.

Try this: FOR AN ALTERNATIVE: 310   FOR ENTERTAINING: 298

Pumpkin–filled Pasta with Butter & Sage

SERVES 6-8

1 quantity ready-made
fresh pasta dough
125 g/4 oz butter
2 tbsp freshly shredded
sage leaves
50 g/2 oz freshly grated
Parmesan cheese,
to serve

For the filling:
250 g/9 oz freshly cooked
pumpkin or sweet potato
flesh, mashed and cooled
75–125 g/3–4 oz dried
breadcrumbs
125 g/4 oz freshly grated
Parmesan cheese

1 medium egg yolk
½ tsp soft brown sugar
2 tbsp freshly chopped
parsley
freshly grated nutmeg
salt and freshly ground
black pepper

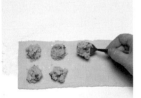

Mix together the ingredients for the filling in a bowl, seasoning to taste with freshly grated nutmeg, salt and pepper. If the mixture seems too wet, add a few more breadcrumbs to bind.

Cut the pasta dough into quarters. Work with one quarter at a time, covering the remaining quarters with a damp tea towel. Roll out a quarter very thinly into a strip 10 cm/4 inches wide. Drop spoonfuls of the filling along the strip 6.5 cm/2½ inches apart, in two rows about 5 cm/2 inches apart. Moisten the outside edges and the spaces between the filling with water. Roll out another strip of pasta and lay it over the filled strip. Press down gently along both edges and between the filled sections. Using a fluted pastry wheel, cut along both long sides, down the centre and between the fillings to form cushions. Transfer the cushions to a lightly floured baking sheet. Continue making cushions and allow to dry for 30 minutes.

Bring a large saucepan of slightly salted water to the boil. Add the pasta cushions and return to the boil. Cook, stirring frequently, for 4–5 minutes, or until 'al dente'. Drain carefully.

Heat the butter in a pan, stir in the shredded sage leaves and cook for 30 seconds. Add the pasta cushions, stir gently then spoon into serving bowls. Sprinkle with the grated Parmesan cheese and serve immediately.

Try this: FOR AN ALTERNATIVE: 292   FOR ENTERTAINING: 258

Tortellini, Cherry Tomato & Mozzarella Skewers

SERVES 6

250 g/9 oz mixed green and plain cheese or vegetable-filled fresh tortellini
150 ml/¼ pint extra virgin olive oil
2 garlic cloves, peeled and crushed
pinch dried thyme or basil
salt and freshly ground black pepper
225 g/8 oz cherry tomatoes
450 g/1 lb mozzarella, cut into 2.5 cm/1 inch cubes
basil leaves, to garnish
dressed salad leaves, to serve

Preheat the grill and line a grill pan with tinfoil, just before cooking. Bring a large pan of lightly salted water to a rolling boil. Add the tortellini and cook according to the packet instructions, or until 'al dente'. Drain, rinse under cold running water, drain again and toss with 2 tablespoons of the olive oil and reserve.

Pour the remaining olive oil into a small bowl. Add the crushed garlic and thyme or basil, then blend well. Season to taste with salt and black pepper and reserve.

To assemble the skewers, thread the tortellini alternately with the cherry tomatoes and cubes of mozzarella. Arrange the skewers on the grill pan and brush generously on all sides with the olive oil mixture.

Cook the skewers under the preheated grill for about 5 minutes, or until they begin to turn golden, turning them halfway through cooking. Arrange two skewers on each plate and garnish with a few basil leaves. Serve immediately with dressed salad leaves.

Try this: FOR AN ALTERNATIVE: 346   FOR ENTERTAINING: 360

Gnocchi Roulade
with Mozzarella & Spinach

SERVES 8

600 ml/1 pint milk
125 g/4 oz fine semolina
  or polenta
25 g/1 oz butter
75 g/3 oz Cheddar
  cheese, grated
2 medium egg yolks

salt and freshly ground
  black pepper
700 g/1½ lb baby spinach
  leaves
½ tsp freshly grated nutmeg
1 garlic clove, peeled and
  crushed

2 tbsp olive oil
150 g/5 oz mozzarella
  cheese, grated
2 tbsp freshly grated
  Parmesan cheese
freshly made tomato sauce,
  to serve

Preheat the oven to 240°C/475°F/Gas Mark 9, 15 minutes before cooking. Oil and line a large Swiss roll tin (23 x 33 cm/9 x 13 inch) with non-stick baking parchment.

Pour the milk into a heavy-based pan and whisk in the semolina. Bring to the boil then simmer, stirring continuously with a wooden spoon, for 3–4 minutes, or until very thick. Remove from heat and stir in the butter and Cheddar cheese until melted. Whisk in the egg yolks and season to taste with salt and pepper. Pour into the lined tin. Cover and allow to cool for 1 hour.

Cook the baby spinach in batches in a large pan with 1 teaspoon of water for 3–4 minutes, or until wilted. Drain thoroughly, season to taste with salt, pepper and nutmeg, then allow to cool. Spread the spinach over the cooled semolina mixture and sprinkle over 75 g/3 oz of the mozzarella and half the Parmesan cheese. Bake in the preheated oven for 20 minutes, or until golden.

Allow to cool, then roll up like a Swiss roll. Sprinkle with the remaining mozzarella and Parmesan cheese, then bake for another 15–20 minutes, or until golden. Serve immediately with freshly made tomato sauce.

  Try this: FOR AN ALTERNATIVE: 154 FOR ENTERTAINING: 156

Cannelloni with Tomato & Red Wine Sauce

SERVES 6

2 tbsp olive oil
1 onion, peeled and
   finely chopped
1 garlic clove, peeled
   and crushed
250 g carton ricotta cheese
50 g/2 oz pine nuts
salt and freshly ground

black pepper
pinch freshly grated nutmeg
250 g/9 oz fresh
   spinach lasagne
25 g/1 oz butter
1 shallot, peeled and
   finely chopped
150 ml/¼ pint red wine

400 g can chopped tomatoes
½ tsp sugar
50 g/2 oz mozzarella cheese,
   grated, plus extra to serve
1 tbsp freshly chopped
   parsley, to garnish
fresh green salad,
   to serve

Preheat the oven to 200°C/400°F/Gas Mark 6, 15 minutes before cooking. Heat the oil in a heavy-based pan, add the onion and garlic and cook for 2–3 minutes. Cool slightly, then stir in the ricotta cheese and pine nuts. Season the filling to taste with salt, pepper and the nutmeg.

Cut each lasagne sheet in half, put a little of the ricotta filling on each piece and roll up like a cigar to resemble cannelloni tubes. Arrange the cannelloni, seam-side down, in a single layer, in a lightly oiled, 2.3 litre/4 pint shallow ovenproof dish.

Melt the butter in a pan, add the shallot and cook for 2 minutes. Pour in the red wine, tomatoes and sugar and season well. Bring to the boil, lower the heat and simmer for about 20 minutes, or until thickened. Add a little more sugar if desired. Transfer to a food processor and blend until a smooth sauce is formed.

Pour the warm tomato sauce over the cannelloni and sprinkle with the grated mozzarella cheese. Bake in the preheated oven for about 30 minutes, or until golden and bubbling. Garnish and serve immediately with a green salad.

Aubergine & Tomato Layer

SERVES 4

2 aubergines, about
   700 g/1½ lb, trimmed
   and thinly sliced
6 tbsp olive oil
1 onion, peeled and
   finely sliced
1 garlic clove, peeled
   and crushed

400 g can chopped tomatoes
50 ml/2 fl oz red wine
½ tsp sugar
salt and freshly ground
   black pepper
50 g/2 oz butter
40 g/1½ oz flour
450 ml/¾ pint milk

225 g/8 oz fresh egg lasagne
2 medium eggs, beaten
200 ml/7 fl oz Greek yogurt
125 g/3 oz mozzarella
   cheese, grated
fresh basil leaves,
   to garnish

Preheat the oven to 190°C/375°F/Gas Mark 5, 10 minutes before cooking. Brush the aubergine slices with 5 tablespoons of the olive oil and place on a baking sheet. Bake in the preheated oven for 20 minutes, or until tender. Remove from the oven and increase the temperature to 200°C/400°F/ Gas Mark 6.

Heat the remaining oil in a heavy-based pan. Add the onion and garlic, cook for 2–3 minutes then add the tomatoes, wine and sugar. Season to taste with salt and pepper, then simmer for 20 minutes.

Melt the butter in another pan. Stir in the flour, cook for 2 minutes, then whisk in the milk. Cook for 2–3 minutes, or until thickened. Season to taste. Pour a little white sauce into a lightly oiled, 1.7 litre/3 pint baking dish. Cover with a layer of lasagne, spread with tomato sauce, then add some of the aubergines. Cover thinly with white sauce and sprinkle with a little cheese. Continue to layer in this way, finishing with a layer of lasagne.

Beat together the eggs and yogurt. Season, then pour over the lasagne. Sprinkle with the remaining cheese and bake in the preheated oven for 25–30 minutes, or until golden. Garnish with basil leaves and serve.

Try this: FOR AN ALTERNATIVE: 302   FOR ENTERTAINING: 280

Ratatouille & Pasta Bake

SERVES 4

1 tbsp olive oil	40 g/1½ oz butter	lasagne
2 large onions, peeled and finely chopped	2 garlic cloves, peeled and crushed	2 large eggs
400 g can chopped tomatoes	125 g/4 oz mushrooms, wiped and thickly sliced	2 tbsp double cream
100 ml/3½ fl oz white wine	700 g/1½ lb courgettes, trimmed and thickly sliced	75 g/3 oz mozzarella cheese, grated
½ tsp caster sugar	125 g/4 oz fresh spinach	25 g/1 oz pecorino cheese, grated
salt and freshly ground black pepper		green salad, to serve

Preheat the oven to 190°C/375°F/Gas Mark 5, 10 minutes before cooking. Heat the olive oil in a heavy-based pan, add half the onion and cook gently for 2–3 minutes. Stir in the tomatoes and wine, then simmer for 20 minutes, or until a thick consistency is formed. Add the sugar and season to taste with salt and pepper. Reserve.

Meanwhile, melt the butter in another pan, add the remaining onion, the garlic, mushrooms and courgettes and cook for 10 minutes, or until softened.

Spread a little tomato sauce in the base of a lightly oiled, 1.4 litre/2 ½ pint baking dish. Top with a layer of lasagne and spoon over half the mushroom and courgette mixture. Repeat the layers, finishing with a layer of lasagne.

Beat the eggs and cream together, then pour over the lasagne. Mix the mozzarella and pecorino cheeses together then sprinkle on top of the lasagne. Place in the preheated oven and cook for 20 minutes, or until golden-brown. Serve immediately with a green salad.

Try this: FOR AN ALTERNATIVE: 220   FOR ENTERTAINING: 28

Baked Macaroni
with Mushrooms & Leeks

SERVES 4

2 tbsp olive oil
1 onion, peeled and
   finely chopped
1 garlic clove, peeled
   and crushed
2 small leeks, trimmed
   and chopped

450 g/1 lb assorted wild
   mushrooms, trimmed
50 ml/2 fl oz white wine
75 g/3 oz butter
150 ml/¼ pint crème fraîche
   or whipping cream
salt and freshly ground

black pepper
75 g/3 oz fresh white
   breadcrumbs
350 g/12 oz short cut
   macaroni
1 tbsp freshly chopped
   parsley, to garnish

Preheat the oven to 220°C/425°F/Gas Mark 7, 15 minutes before cooking. Heat 1 tablespoon of the olive oil in a large frying pan, add the onion and garlic and cook for 2 minutes. Add the leeks, mushrooms and 25 g/1 oz of the butter then cook for 5 minutes. Pour in the white wine, cook for 2 minutes then stir in the crème fraîche or cream. Season to taste with salt and pepper.

Meanwhile, bring a large pan of lightly salted water to a rolling boil. Add the macaroni and cook according to the packet instructions, or until 'al dente'.

Melt 25 g/1 oz of the butter with the remaining oil in a small frying pan. Add the breadcrumbs and fry until just beginning to turn golden-brown. Drain on absorbent kitchen paper.

Drain the pasta thoroughly, toss in the remaining butter then tip into a lightly oiled, 1.4 litre/2½ pint shallow baking dish. Cover the pasta with the leek and mushroom mixture then sprinkle with the fried breadcrumbs. Bake in the preheated oven for 5–10 minutes, or until golden and crisp. Garnish with chopped parsley and serve.

Try this: FOR AN ALTERNATIVE: 306   FOR ENTERTAINING: 44

Baby Roast Potato Salad

SERVES 4

350 g/12 oz small shallots
sea salt and freshly ground
   black pepper
900 g/2 lb small even-sized
   new potatoes

2 tbsp olive oil
2 medium courgettes
2 sprigs of fresh rosemary
175 g/6 oz cherry tomatoes
150 ml/¼ pint soured cream

2 tbsp freshly
   snipped chives
¼ tsp paprika

Preheat the oven to 200°C/400°F/Gas Mark 6. Trim the shallots, but leave the skins on. Put in a saucepan of lightly salted boiling water with the potatoes and cook for 5 minutes, then drain. Separate the shallots and plunge them into cold water for 1 minute.

Put the oil in a baking sheet lined with tinfoil or roasting tin and heat for a few minutes. Peel the skins off the shallots – they should now come away easily. Add to the baking sheet or roasting tin with the potatoes and toss in the oil to coat. Sprinkle with a little sea salt. Roast the potatoes and shallots in the preheated oven for 10 minutes.

Meanwhile, trim the courgettes, halve lengthways and cut into 5 cm/2 inch chunks. Add to the baking sheet or roasting tin, toss to mix and cook for 5 minutes.

Pierce the tomato skins with a sharp knife. Add to the sheet or tin with the rosemary and cook for a further 5 minutes, or until all the vegetables are tender. Remove the rosemary and discard. Grind a little black pepper over the vegetables.

Spoon into a wide serving bowl. Mix together the soured cream and chives and drizzle over the vegetables just before serving.

Try this: FOR AN ALTERNATIVE: 40   FOR ENTERTAINING: 82

Oriental Noodle & Peanut Salad with Coriander

SERVES 4

350 g/12 oz rice vermicelli
1 litre/1¾ pints light
    vegetable stock
2 tsp sesame oil
2 tbsp light soy sauce
8 spring onions

3 tbsp groundnut oil
2 hot green chillis, deseeded
    and thinly sliced
25 g/1 oz roughly
    chopped coriander
2 tbsp freshly chopped mint

125 g/4 oz cucumber,
    finely chopped
40 g/1½ oz beansprouts
40 g/1½ oz roasted peanuts,
    roughly chopped

Put the noodles into a large bowl. Bring the stock to the boil and immediately pour over the noodles. Leave to soak for 4 minutes, or according to the packet directions. Drain well, discarding the stock or saving it for another use. Mix together the sesame oil and soy sauce and pour over the hot noodles. Toss well to coat and leave until cold.

Trim and thinly slice four of the spring onions. Heat the oil in a wok over a low heat. Add the spring onions and, as soon as they sizzle, remove from the heat and leave to cool. When cold, toss with the noodles.

On a chopping board, cut the remaining spring onions lengthways four to six times, then leave in a bowl of cold water until tassels form. Serve the noodles in individual bowls, each dressed with a little chilli, coriander, mint, cucumber, beansprouts and peanuts. Garnish with the spring onion tassels and serve.

Try this: FOR AN ALTERNATIVE: 48   FOR ENTERTAINING: 116

Warm Noodle Salad with Sesame & Peanut Dressing

SERVES 4-6

125 g/4 oz smooth
   peanut butter
6 tbsp sesame oil
3 tbsp light soy sauce
2 tbsp red wine vinegar
1 tbsp freshly grated
   root ginger

2 tbsp double cream
250 g pack Chinese fine
   egg noodles
125 g/4 oz beansprouts
225 g/8 oz baby sweetcorn
125 g/4 oz carrots, peeled
   and cut into matchsticks

125 g/4 oz mangetout
125 g/4 oz cucumber,
   cut into thin strips
3 spring onions, trimmed
   and finely shredded

Place the peanut butter, 4 tablespoons of the sesame oil, the soy sauce, vinegar and ginger in a food processor. Blend until smooth, then stir in 75 ml/3 fl oz hot water and blend again. Pour in the cream, blend briefly until smooth. Pour the dressing into a jug and reserve.

Bring a saucepan of lightly salted water to the boil, add the noodles and beansprouts and cook for 4 minutes or according to the packet instructions. Drain, rinse under cold running water and drain again. Stir in the remaining sesame oil and keep warm.

Bring a saucepan of lightly salted water to the boil and add the baby sweetcorn, carrots and mangetout and cook for 3–4 minutes, or until just tender but still crisp. Drain and cut the mangetout in half. Slice the baby sweetcorn (if very large) into two to three pieces and arrange on a warmed serving dish with the noodles. Add the cucumber strips and spring onions. Spoon over a little of the dressing and serve immediately with the remaining dressing.

Try this: FOR AN ALTERNATIVE: 340 FOR ENTERTAINING: 356

Spicy Cucumber Stir Fry

SERVES 4

25 g/1 oz black soya beans, soaked in cold water overnight
1½ cucumbers
2 tsp salt

1 tbsp groundnut oil
½ tsp mild chilli powder
4 garlic cloves, peeled and crushed
5 tbsp vegetable stock

1 tsp sesame oil
1 tbsp freshly chopped parsley, to garnish

Rinse the soaked beans thoroughly, then drain. Place in a saucepan, cover with cold water and bring to the boil, skimming off any scum that rises to the surface. Boil for 10 minutes, then reduce the heat and simmer for 1–1½ hours. Drain and reserve.

Peel the cucumbers, slice lengthways and remove the seeds. Cut into 2.5 cm/1 inch slices and place in a colander over a bowl. Sprinkle the salt over the cucumber and leave for 30 minutes. Rinse thoroughly in cold water, drain and pat dry with absorbent kitchen paper.

Heat a wok or large frying pan, add the oil and when hot, add the chilli powder, garlic and black beans and stir-fry for 30 seconds. Add the cucumber and stir-fry for 20 seconds.

Pour the stock into the wok and cook for 3–4 minutes, or until the cucumber is very tender. The liquid will have evaporated at this stage. Remove from the heat and stir in the sesame oil. Turn into a warmed serving dish, garnish with chopped parsley and serve immediately.

Try this FOR AN ALTERNATIVE: 342 FOR ENTERTAINING: 84

Chinese Egg Fried Rice

SERVES 4

250 g/9 oz long-grain rice
1 tbsp dark sesame oil
2 large eggs
1 tbsp sunflower oil
2 garlic cloves, peeled
  and crushed
2.5 cm/1 inch piece fresh
  root ginger, peeled

and grated
1 carrot, peeled and cut
  into matchsticks
125 g/4 oz mangetout,
  halved
220 g can water chestnuts,
  drained and halved
1 yellow pepper, deseeded

and diced
4 spring onions, trimmed
  and finely shredded
2 tbsp light soy sauce
½ tsp paprika
salt and freshly ground
  black pepper

Bring a saucepan of lightly salted water to the boil, add the rice and cook for 15 minutes or according to the packet instructions. Drain and leave to cool.

Heat a wok or large frying pan and add the sesame oil. Beat the eggs in a small bowl and pour into the hot wok. Using a fork, draw the egg in from the sides of the pan to the centre until it sets, then turn over and cook the other side. When set and golden turn out on to a board. Leave to cool, then cut into very thin strips.

Wipe the wok clean with absorbent kitchen paper, return to the heat and add the sunflower oil. When hot add the garlic and ginger and stir-fry for 30 seconds. Add the remaining vegetables and continue to stir-fry for 3–4 minutes, or until tender but still crisp.

Stir the reserved cooked rice into the wok with the soy sauce and paprika and season to taste with salt and pepper. Fold in the cooked egg strips and heat through. Tip into a warmed serving dish and serve immediately.

Try this: FOR AN ALTERNATIVE: 358 FOR ENTERTAINING: 354

Vegetable Tempura

SERVES 4-6

125 g/4 oz rice flour
75 g/3 oz plain flour
4 tsp baking powder
1 tbsp dried mustard powder
2 tsp semolina
salt and freshly ground

black pepper
300 ml/½ pint groundnut oil
125 g/4 oz courgette,
    trimmed and thickly sliced
125 g/4 oz mangetout
125 g/4 oz baby sweetcorn

4 small red onions, peeled
    and quartered
1 large red pepper, deseeded
    and cut into 2.5 cm/1 inch
    wide strips
light soy sauce, to serve

Sift the rice flour and the plain flour into a large bowl, then sift in the baking powder and dried mustard powder.

Stir the semolina into the flour mixture and season to taste with salt and pepper. Gradually beat in 300 ml/½ pint cold water to produce a thin coating batter. Leave to stand at room temperature for 30 minutes.

Heat a wok or large frying pan, add the oil and heat to 180°C/350°F. Working in batches and using a slotted spoon, dip the vegetables in the batter until well coated, then drop them carefully into the hot oil. Cook each batch for 2–3 minutes or until golden. Drain on absorbent kitchen paper and keep warm while cooking the remaining batches.

Transfer the vegetables to a warmed serving platter and serve immediately with the light soy sauce to use as a dipping sauce.

Try this: FOR AN ALTERNATIVE: 360   FOR ENTERTAINING: 346

Thai–style Cauliflower & Potato Curry

SERVES 4

450 g/1 lb new potatoes, peeled and halved or quartered
350 g/12 oz cauliflower florets
3 garlic cloves, peeled and crushed
1 onion, peeled and finely chopped

40 g/1½ oz ground almonds
1 tsp ground coriander
½ tsp ground cumin
½ tsp turmeric
3 tbsp groundnut oil
salt and freshly ground black pepper
50 g/2 oz creamed coconut, broken into small pieces

200 ml/7 fl oz vegetable stock
1 tbsp mango chutney
sprigs of fresh coriander, to garnish
freshly cooked long-grain rice, to serve

Bring a saucepan of lightly salted water to the boil, add the potatoes and cook for 15 minutes or until just tender. Drain and leave to cool. Boil the cauliflower for 2 minutes, then drain and refresh under cold running water. Drain again and reserve.

Meanwhile, blend the garlic, onion, ground almonds and spices with 2 tablespoons of the oil and salt and pepper to taste in a food processor until a smooth paste is formed. Heat a wok, add the remaining oil and when hot, add the spice paste and cook for 3–4 minutes, stirring continuously.

Dissolve the creamed coconut in 6 tablespoons of boiling water and add to the wok. Pour in the stock, cook for 2–3 minutes, then stir in the cooked potatoes and cauliflower.

Stir in the mango chutney and heat through for 3–4 minutes or until piping hot. Tip into a warmed serving dish, garnish with sprigs of fresh coriander and serve immediately with freshly cooked rice.

Try this: FOR AN ALTERNATIVE: 368   FOR ENTERTAINING: 378

Coconut–baked Courgettes

SERVES 4

3 tbsp groundnut oil
1 onion, peeled and
   finely sliced
4 garlic cloves,
   peeled and crushed

½ tsp chilli powder
1 tsp ground coriander
6–8 tbsp desiccated coconut
1 tbsp tomato purée
700 g/1½ lb courgettes,

thinly sliced
freshly chopped parsley,
   to garnish

Preheat the oven to 180°C/350°F/Gas Mark 4, 10 minutes before cooking. Lightly oil a 1.4 litre/2½ pint ovenproof gratin dish. Heat a wok, add the oil and when hot, add the onion and stir-fry for 2–3 minutes or until softened. Add the garlic, chilli powder and coriander and stir-fry for 1–2 minutes.

Pour 300 ml/½ pint cold water into the wok and bring to the boil. Add the coconut and tomato purée and simmer for 3–4 minutes; most of the water will evaporate at this stage. Spoon 4 tablespoons of the spice and coconut mixture into a small bowl and reserve.

Stir the courgettes into the remaining spice and coconut mixture, coating well. Spoon the courgettes into the oiled gratin dish and sprinkle the reserved spice and coconut mixture evenly over the top. Bake, uncovered, in the preheated oven for 15–20 minutes, or until golden. Garnish with chopped parsley and serve immediately.

Try this: FOR AN ALTERNATIVE: 260   FOR ENTERTAINING: 306

Vegetarian

Cooked Vegetable Salad with Satay Sauce

SERVES 4

125 ml/4 fl oz groundnut oil
225 g/8 oz unsalted peanuts
1 onion, peeled and
  finely chopped
1 garlic clove, peeled
  and crushed
½ tsp chilli powder
1 tsp ground coriander
½ tsp ground cumin
½ tsp sugar

1 tbsp dark soy sauce
2 tbsp fresh lemon juice
2 tbsp light olive oil
salt and freshly ground
  black pepper
125 g/4 oz French
  green beans, trimmed
  and halved
125 g/4 oz carrots
125 g/4 oz cauliflower florets

125 g/4 oz broccoli florets
125 g/4 oz Chinese leaves or
  pak choi, trimmed and
  shredded
125 g/4 oz beansprouts
1 tbsp sesame oil

To garnish:
sprigs of fresh watercress
cucumber, cut into slivers

Heat a wok, add the oil, and when hot, add the peanuts and stir-fry for 3–4 minutes. Drain on absorbent kitchen paper and leave to cool. Blend in a food processor to a fine powder.

Place the onion and garlic, with the spices, sugar, soy sauce, lemon juice and olive oil in a food processor. Season to taste with salt and pepper, then process into a paste. Transfer to a wok and stir-fry for 3–4 minutes.

Stir 600 ml/1 pint hot water into the paste and bring to the boil. Add the ground peanuts and simmer gently for 5–6 minutes or until the mixture thickens. Reserve the satay sauce.

Cook in batches in lightly salted boiling water. Cook the French beans, carrots, cauliflower and broccoli for 3–4 minutes, and the Chinese leaves or pak choi and beansprouts for 2 minutes. Drain each batch, drizzle over the sesame oil and arrange on a large warmed serving dish. Garnish with watercress sprigs and cucumber. Serve with the satay sauce.

Try this: FOR AN ALTERNATIVE: 328   FOR ENTERTAINING: 308

Mixed Vegetables Stir Fry

SERVES 4

2 tbsp groundnut oil
4 garlic cloves, peeled and
    finely sliced
2.5 cm/1 inch piece fresh
    root ginger, peeled and
    finely sliced
75 g/3 oz broccoli florets
50 g/2 oz mangetout,

trimmed
75 g/3 oz carrots, peeled and
    cut into matchsticks
1 green pepper, deseeded
    and cut into strips
1 red pepper, deseeded and
    cut into strips
1 tbsp soy sauce

1 tbsp hoisin sauce
1 tsp sugar
salt and freshly ground
    black pepper
4 spring onions, trimmed
    and shredded, to garnish

Heat a wok, add the oil and when hot, add the garlic and ginger slices and stir-fry for 1 minute.

Add the broccoli florets to the wok, stir-fry for 1 minute, then add the mangetout, carrots and the green and red peppers and stir-fry for a further 3–4 minutes, or until tender but still crisp.

Blend the soy sauce, hoisin sauce and sugar in a small bowl. Stir well, season to taste with salt and pepper and pour into the wok.

Transfer the vegetables to a warmed serving dish. Garnish with shredded spring onions and serve immediately.

Try this: FOR AN ALTERNATIVE: 334   FOR ENTERTAINING: 340

Savoury Wontons

MAKES 15

125 g/4 oz filo pastry or wonton skins
15 whole chive leaves
225 g/8 oz spinach
25 g/1 oz butter
1/2 tsp salt
225 g/8 oz mushrooms, wiped and roughly chopped
1 garlic clove, peeled and crushed
1–2 tbsp dark soy sauce
2.5 cm/1 inch piece fresh root ginger, peeled and grated
salt and freshly ground black pepper
1 small egg, beaten
300 ml/½ pint groundnut oil for deep-frying

To garnish:
spring onion curls
radish roses

Cut the filo pastry or wonton skins into 12.5 cm/5 inch squares, stack and cover with clingfilm. Chill in the refrigerator while preparing the filling. Blanch the chive leaves in boiling water for 1 minute, drain and reserve.

Melt the butter in a saucepan, add the spinach and salt and cook for 2–3 minutes or until wilted. Add the mushrooms and garlic and cook for 2–3 minutes or until tender. Transfer the spinach and mushroom mixture to a bowl. Stir in the soy sauce and ginger. Season to taste with salt and pepper.

Place a small spoonful of the spinach and mushroom mixture on to a pastry or wonton square and brush the edges with beaten egg. Gather up the four corners to make a little bag and tie with a chive leaf. Make up the remainder of the wontons.

Heat a wok, add the oil and heat to 180°C/350°F. Deep-fry the wontons in batches for 2–3 minutes, or until golden and crisp. Drain on absorbent kitchen paper and serve immediately, garnished with spring onion curls and radish roses.

Try this: FOR AN ALTERNATIVE: 354   FOR ENTERTAINING: 360

Corn Fritters with Hot & Spicy Relish

MAKES 16-20

325 g can sweetcorn
  kernels, drained
1 onion, peeled and very
  finely chopped
1 spring onion, trimmed and
  very finely chopped
½ tsp chilli powder
1 tsp ground coriander

4 tbsp plain flour
1 tsp baking powder
1 medium egg
salt and freshly ground
  black pepper
300 ml/½ pint groundnut oil
sprigs of fresh coriander,
  to garnish

For the spicy relish:
3 tbsp sunflower oil
1 onion, peeled and very
  finely chopped
¼ tsp dried crushed chillies
2 garlic cloves, peeled
  and crushed
2 tbsp plum sauce

Make the relish. Heat a wok, add the sunflower oil and when hot, add the onion and stir-fry for 3–4 minutes or until softened. Add the chillies and garlic, stir-fry for 1 minute, then leave to cool slightly. Stir in the plum sauce, transfer to a food processor and blend until the consistency of chutney. Reserve.

Place the sweetcorn into a food processor and blend briefly until just mashed. Transfer to a bowl with the onions, chilli powder, coriander, flour, baking powder and egg. Season to taste with salt and pepper and mix together.

Heat a wok, add the oil and heat to 180°C/350°F. Working in batches, drop a few spoonfuls of the sweetcorn mixture into the oil and deep-fry for 3–4 minutes, or until golden and crispy, turning occasionally. Using a slotted spoon, remove and drain on absorbent kitchen paper. Arrange on a warmed serving platter, garnish with sprigs of coriander and serve immediately with the relish.

Try this: FOR AN ALTERNATIVE: 312   FOR ENTERTAINING: 168

Chinese Leaves with Sweet & Sour Sauce

SERVES 4

1 head Chinese leaves	2 tbsp brown sugar	3 tbsp sunflower oil
200 g pack pak choi	3 tbsp red wine vinegar	15 g/½ oz butter
1 tbsp cornflour	3 tbsp orange juice	1 tsp salt
1 tbsp soy sauce	2 tbsp tomato purée	2 tbsp toasted sesame seeds

Discard any tough outer leaves and stalks from the Chinese leaves and pak choi and wash well. Drain thoroughly and pat dry with absorbent kitchen paper. Shred the Chinese leaves and pak choi lengthways. Reserve.

In a small bowl, blend the cornflour with 4 tablespoons of water. Add the soy sauce, sugar, vinegar, orange juice and tomato purée and stir until blended thoroughly.

Pour the sauce into a small saucepan and bring to the boil. Simmer gently for 2–3 minutes, or until the sauce is thickened and smooth.

Meanwhile, heat a wok or large frying pan and add the sunflower oil and butter. When melted, add the prepared Chinese leaves and pak choi, sprinkle with the salt and stir-fry for 2 minutes. Reduce the heat and cook gently for a further 1–2 minutes or until tender.

Transfer the Chinese leaves and pak choi to a warmed serving platter and drizzle over the warm sauce. Sprinkle with the toasted sesame seeds and serve immediately.

Try this: FOR AN ALTERNATIVE: 342   FOR ENTERTAINING: 366

Bean & Cashew Stir Fry

SERVES 4

3 tbsp sunflower oil
1 onion, peeled and
   finely chopped
1 celery stalk, trimmed
   and chopped
2.5 cm/1 inch piece fresh
   root ginger, peeled
   and grated
2 garlic cloves, peeled

   and crushed
1 red chilli, deseeded and
   finely chopped
175 g/6 oz fine French beans,
   trimmed and halved
175 g/6 oz mangetout, sliced
   diagonally into 3
75 g/3 oz unsalted
   cashew nuts

1 tsp brown sugar
125 ml/4 fl oz vegetable stock
2 tbsp dry sherry
1 tbsp light soy sauce
1 tsp red wine vinegar
salt and freshly ground
   black pepper
freshly chopped coriander,
   to garnish

Heat a wok or large frying pan, add the oil and when hot, add the onion and celery and stir-fry gently for 3–4 minutes or until softened.

Add the ginger, garlic and chilli to the wok and stir-fry for 30 seconds. Stir in the French beans and mangetout together with the cashew nuts and continue to stir-fry for 1–2 minutes, or until the nuts are golden brown.

Dissolve the sugar in the stock, then blend with the sherry, soy sauce and vinegar. Stir into the bean mixture and bring to the boil. Simmer gently, stirring occasionally for 3–4 minutes, or until the beans and mangetout are tender but still crisp and the sauce has thickened slightly.

Season to taste with salt and pepper. Transfer to a warmed serving bowl or spoon on to individual plates. Sprinkle with freshly chopped coriander and serve immediately.

Try this: FOR AN ALTERNATIVE: 352   FOR ENTERTAINING: 364

Fried Rice with Bamboo Shoots & Ginger

SERVES 4

4 tbsp sunflower oil
1 onion, peeled and
    finely chopped
225 g/8 oz long-grain rice
3 garlic cloves, peeled and
    cut into slivers
2.5 cm/1 inch piece fresh
    root ginger, peeled
    and grated

3 spring onions, trimmed
    and chopped
450 ml/¾ pint
    vegetable stock
125 g/4 oz button
    mushrooms, wiped
    and halved
75 g/3 oz frozen peas,
    thawed

2 tbsp light soy sauce
500 g can bamboo shoots,
    drained and thinly sliced
salt and freshly ground
    black pepper
cayenne pepper, to taste
fresh coriander leaves,
    to garnish

Heat a wok, add the oil and when hot, add the onion and cook gently for 3–4 minutes, then add the long-grain rice and cook for 3–4 minutes or until golden, stirring frequently.

Add the garlic, ginger and chopped spring onions to the wok and stir well. Pour the vegetable stock into a small saucepan and bring to the boil. Carefully ladle the hot stock into the wok, stir well, then simmer gently for 10 minutes or until most of the liquid has been absorbed.

Stir the button mushrooms, peas and soy sauce into the wok and continue to cook for a further 5 minutes, or until the rice is tender, adding a little extra stock if necessary.

Add the bamboo shoots to the wok and carefully stir in. Season to taste with salt, pepper and cayenne pepper. Cook for 2–3 minutes or until heated through. Tip on to a warmed serving dish, garnish with coriander leaves and serve immediately.

Try this: FOR AN ALTERNATIVE: 362   FOR ENTERTAINING: 372

Spring Rolls with Mixed Vegetables

MAKES 12

2 tbsp sesame oil
125 g/4 oz broccoli florets,
  cut into small pieces
125 g/4 oz carrots, peeled
  and cut into matchsticks
125 g/4 oz courgettes, cut
  into strips
150 g/5 oz button
  mushrooms, finely

chopped
2.5 cm/1 inch piece fresh
  root ginger, peeled
  and grated
1 garlic clove, peeled and
  finely chopped
4 spring onions, trimmed
  and finely chopped
75 g/3 oz beansprouts

1 tbsp light soy sauce
pinch of cayenne pepper
4 tbsp plain flour
12 sheets filo pastry
300 ml/½ pint groundnut oil
spring onion curls,
  to garnish

Heat a wok, add the sesame oil and when hot, add the broccoli, carrots, courgettes, mushrooms, ginger, garlic and spring onions and stir-fry for 1–2 minutes, or until slightly softened.

Turn into a bowl, add the beansprouts, soy sauce and cayenne pepper and mix together. Transfer the vegetables to a colander and drain for 5 minutes. Meanwhile, blend the flour with 2–3 tablespoons of water to form a paste and reserve.

Fold a sheet of filo pastry in half and in half again, brushing a little water between each layer. Place a spoonful of the drained vegetable mixture on the pastry. Brush a little of the flour paste along the edges. Turn the edges into the centre, then roll up and seal. Repeat with the rest.

Wipe the wok clean, return to the heat, add the oil and heat to 190˚C/375˚F. Add the spring rolls in batches and deep-fry for 2–3 minutes, or until golden. Drain on absorbent kitchen paper, arrange on a platter, garnish with spring onion curls and serve immediately.

Try this: FOR AN ALTERNATIVE: 360 FOR ENTERTAINING: 228

Indonesian Salad with Peanut Dressing

SERVES 4

225 g/8 oz new potatoes, scrubbed
1 large carrot, peeled and cut into matchsticks
125 g/4 oz French beans, trimmed
225 g/8 oz tiny cauliflower florets
125 g/4 oz cucumber, cut

into matchsticks
75 g/3 oz fresh bean sprouts
3 medium eggs, hard-boiled and quartered

For the peanut dressing:
2 tbsp sesame oil
1 garlic clove, peeled and crushed

1 red chilli, deseeded and finely chopped
150 g/5 oz crunchy peanut butter
6 tbsp hot vegetable stock
2 tsp soft light brown sugar
2 tsp dark soy sauce
1 tbsp lime juice

Cook the potatoes in a saucepan of boiling salted water for 15–20 minutes until tender. Remove with a slotted spoon and thickly slice into a large bowl. Keep the saucepan of water boiling.

Add the carrot, French beans and cauliflower to the water, return to the boil and cook for 2 minutes, or until just tender. Drain and refresh under cold running water, then drain well. Add to the potatoes with the cucumber and bean sprouts.

To make the dressing, gently heat the sesame oil in a small saucepan. Add the garlic and chilli and cook for a few seconds, then remove from the heat. Stir in the peanut butter.

Stir in the stock, a little at a time. Add the remaining ingredients and mix together to make a thick, creamy dressing.

Divide the vegetables between four plates and arrange the eggs on top. Drizzle the dressing over the salad and serve immediately.

Try this: FOR AN ALTERNATIVE: 380   FOR ENTERTAINING: 80

Chinese Omelette

SERVES 1

50 g/2 oz beansprouts
50 g/2 oz carrots, peeled and
  cut into matchsticks
1 cm/½ inch piece fresh root
  ginger, peeled and grated

1 tsp soy sauce
2 large eggs
salt and freshly ground
  black pepper
1 tbsp dark sesame oil

To serve:
tossed green salad
egg fried rice (see
  page 332)
soy sauce

Lightly rinse the beansprouts, then place in the top of a bamboo steamer with the carrots. Add the grated ginger and soy sauce. Set the steamer over a pan or wok half-filled with gently simmering water and steam for 10 minutes, or until the vegetables are tender but still crisp. Reserve and keep warm.

Whisk the eggs in a bowl until frothy and season to taste with salt and pepper. Heat a 20.5 cm/8 inch omelette or frying pan, add the sesame oil and when very hot, pour in the beaten eggs. Whisk the eggs around with a fork, then allow them to cook and start to set. When the top surface starts to bubble, tilt the edges to allow the uncooked egg to run underneath.

Spoon the beansprout and carrot mixture over the top of the omelette and allow it to cook a little longer. When it has set, slide the omelette on to a warmed serving dish and carefully roll up. Serve immediately with a tossed green salad, egg fried rice and extra soy sauce.

 Try this: FOR AN ALTERNATIVE: 98   FOR ENTERTAINING: 114

Crispy Pancake Rolls

SERVES 4

250 g/9 oz plain flour
pinch of salt
1 medium egg
4 tsp sunflower oil
2 tbsp light olive oil
2 cm/¾ inch piece fresh root
   ginger, peeled and grated
1 garlic clove, peeled

and crushed
225 g/8 oz tofu, drained and
   cut into small dice
2 tbsp soy sauce
1 tbsp dry sherry
175 g/6 oz button
   mushrooms, wiped
   and chopped

1 celery stalk, trimmed and
   finely chopped
2 spring onions, trimmed
   and finely chopped
2 tbsp groundnut oil
fresh coriander sprig and
   sliced spring onion,
   to garnish

Sift 225 g/8 oz of the flour with the salt into a large bowl, make a well in the centre and drop in the egg. Beat to form a smooth, thin batter, gradually adding 300 ml/½ pint of water and drawing in the flour from the sides of the bowl. Mix the remaining flour with 1–2 tablespoons of water to make a thick paste. Reserve.

Heat a little sunflower oil in a 20.5 cm/8 inch omelette or frying pan and pour in 2 tablespoons of the batter. Cook for 1–2 minutes, flip over and cook for a further 1–2 minutes, or until firm. Slide from the pan and keep warm. Make more pancakes with the remaining batter.

Heat a wok or large frying pan, add the olive oil and when hot, add the ginger, garlic and tofu, stir-fry for 30 seconds, then pour in the soy sauce and sherry. Add the mushrooms, celery and spring onions. Stir-fry for 1–2 minutes, then remove from the wok and leave to cool.

Place a little filling in the centre of each pancake. Brush the edges, with the flour paste, fold in the edges, then roll up into parcels. Heat the groundnut oil to 180°C/350°F in the wok. Fry the pancake rolls for 2–3 minutes or until golden. Serve immediately, garnished with chopped spring onions and a sprig of coriander.

Vegetables in Coconut Milk with Rice Noodles

SERVES 4

75 g/3 oz creamed coconut
1 tsp salt
2 tbsp sunflower oil
2 garlic cloves, peeled and finely chopped
2 red peppers, deseeded and

cut into thin strips
2.5 cm/1 inch piece of fresh root ginger, peeled and cut into thin strips
125 g/4 oz baby sweetcorn
2 tsp cornflour

2 medium ripe but still firm avocados
1 small Cos lettuce, cut into thick strips
freshly cooked rice noodles, to serve

Roughly chop the creamed coconut, place in a bowl with the salt, then pour over 600 ml/1 pint of boiling water. Stir until the coconut has dissolved completely and reserve.

Heat a wok or large frying pan, add the oil and when hot, add the chopped garlic, sliced peppers and ginger. Cook for 30 seconds, then cover and cook very gently for 10 minutes or until the peppers are soft.

Pour in the reserved coconut milk and bring to the boil. Stir in the baby sweetcorn, cover and simmer for 5 minutes. Blend the cornflour with 2 teaspoons of water, pour into the wok and cook, stirring, for 2 minutes or until thickened slightly.

Cut the avocados in half, peel, remove the stone and slice. Add to the wok with the lettuce strips and stir until well mixed and heated through. Serve immediately on a bed of rice noodles.

Thai Fried Noodles

SERVES 4

450 g/1 lb tofu
2 tbsp dry sherry
125 g/4 oz medium
   egg noodles
125 g/4 oz mangetout,
   halved
3 tbsp groundnut oil
1 onion, peeled and
   finely sliced

1 garlic clove, peeled and
   finely sliced
2.5 cm/1 inch piece fresh
   root ginger, peeled and
   finely sliced
125 g/4 oz beansprouts
1 tbsp Thai fish sauce
2 tbsp light soy sauce
½ tsp sugar

salt and freshly ground
   black pepper
½ courgette, cut into
   matchsticks

To garnish:
2 tbsp roasted peanuts,
   roughly chopped
sprigs of fresh basil

Cut the tofu into cubes and place in a bowl. Sprinkle over the sherry and toss to coat. Cover loosely and leave to marinate in the refrigerator for 30 minutes.

Bring a large saucepan of lightly salted water to the boil and add the noodles and mangetout. Simmer for 3 minutes or according to the packet instructions, then drain and rinse under cold running water. Leave to drain again.

Heat a wok or large frying pan, add the oil and when hot, add the onion and stir-fry for 2–3 minutes. Add the garlic and ginger and stir-fry for 30 seconds. Add the beansprouts and tofu, stir in the Thai fish sauce and the soy sauce with the sugar and season to taste with salt and pepper.

Stir-fry the tofu mixture over a medium heat for 2–3 minutes, then add the courgettes, noodles and mangetout and stir-fry for a further 1–2 minutes. Tip into a warmed serving dish or spoon on to individual plates. Sprinkle with the peanuts, add a sprig of basil and serve immediately.

Try this: FOR AN ALTERNATIVE: 370 FOR ENTERTAINING: 342

Stir-fried Greens

SERVES 4

450 g/1 lb Chinese leaves
225 g/8 oz pak choi
225 g/8 oz broccoli florets
1 tbsp sesame seeds
1 tbsp groundnut oil
1 tbsp fresh root ginger,
    peeled and finely chopped

3 garlic cloves, peeled
    and finely chopped
2 red chillies, deseeded
    and split in half
50 ml/2 fl oz vegetable stock
2 tbsp Chinese rice wine
1 tbsp dark soy sauce

1 tsp light soy sauce
2 tsp black bean sauce
freshly ground black pepper
2 tsp sugar
1 tsp sesame oil

Separate the Chinese leaves and pak choi and wash well. Cut into 2.5 cm/1 inch strips. Separate the broccoli into small florets. Heat a wok or large frying pan, add the sesame seeds and stir-fry for 30 seconds or until browned.

Add the oil to the wok and when hot, add the ginger, garlic and chillies and stir-fry for 30 seconds. Add the broccoli and stir-fry for 1 minute. Add the Chinese leaves and pak choi and stir-fry for a further 1 minute.

Pour the vegetable stock and Chinese rice wine into the wok with the soy and black bean sauces. Season to taste with pepper and add the sugar. Reduce the heat and simmer for 6–8 minutes, or until the vegetables are tender but still firm to the bite.

Tip into a warmed serving dish, removing the chillies if preferred. Drizzle with the sesame oil and serve immediately.

Try this: FOR AN ALTERNATIVE: 330   FOR ENTERTAINING: 340

Vegetable Kofta Curry

SERVES 6

350 g/12 oz potatoes, peeled and diced
225 g/8 oz carrots, peeled and roughly chopped
225 g/8 oz parsnips, peeled and roughly chopped
1 medium egg, lightly beaten
75 g/3 oz plain flour, sifted

8 tbsp sunflower oil
2 onions, peeled and sliced
2 garlic cloves, peeled and crushed
2.5 cm/1 inch piece fresh root ginger, peeled and grated
2 tbsp garam masala
2 tbsp tomato paste

300 ml/½ pint vegetable stock
250 ml/9 fl oz Greek style yogurt
3 tbsp freshly chopped coriander
salt and freshly ground black pepper

Bring a saucepan of lightly salted water to the boil. Add the potatoes, carrots and parsnips. Cover and simmer for 12–15 minutes, or until the vegetables are tender. Drain the vegetables and mash until very smooth. Stir the egg into the vegetable purée, then add the flour and mix to make a stiff paste and reserve.

Heat 2 tablespoons of the oil in a wok and gently cook the onions for 10 minutes. Add the garlic and ginger and cook for a further 2–3 minutes, or until very soft and just beginning to colour. Sprinkle the garam masala over the onions and stir in. Add the tomato paste and stock. Bring to the boil, cover and simmer gently for 15 minutes.

Meanwhile, heat the remaining oil in a wok or frying pan. Drop in tablespoons of vegetable batter, four or five at a time and fry, turning often, for 3–4 minutes until brown and crisp. Remove with a slotted spoon and drain on absorbent kitchen paper. Keep warm in a low oven while cooking the rest. Stir the yogurt and coriander into the onion sauce. Slowly heat to boiling point and season to taste with salt and pepper. Divide the koftas between warmed serving plates and spoon over the sauce. Serve immediately.

Thai Noodles & Vegetables with Tofu

SERVES 4

225 g/8 oz firm tofu
2 tbsp soy sauce
rind of 1 lime, grated
2 lemon grass stalks
1 red chilli
1 litre/1¾ pint
   vegetable stock
2 slices fresh root
  ginger, peeled

2 garlic cloves, peeled
2 sprigs of fresh coriander
175 g/6 oz dried thread
   egg noodles
125 g/4 oz shiitake or button
   mushrooms, sliced
   if large
2 carrots, peeled and
   cut into matchsticks

125 g/4 oz mangetout
125 g/4 oz bok choy or
   other Chinese leaf
1 tbsp freshly
   chopped coriander
salt and freshly ground
   black pepper
coriander sprigs, to garnish

Drain the tofu well and cut into cubes. Put into a shallow dish with the soy sauce and lime rind. Stir well to coat and leave to marinate for 30 minutes.

Meanwhile, put the lemon grass and chilli on a chopping board and bruise with the side of a large knife, ensuring the blade is pointing away from you. Put the vegetable stock in a large saucepan and add the lemon grass, chilli, ginger, garlic, and coriander. Bring to the boil, cover and simmer gently for 20 minutes.

Strain the stock into a clean pan. Return to the boil and add the noodles, tofu and its marinade and the mushrooms. Simmer gently for 4 minutes.

Add the carrots, mangetout, bok choy, coriander and simmer for a further 3–4 minutes until the vegetables are just tender. Season to taste with salt and pepper. Garnish with coriander sprigs. Serve immediately.

Try this: FOR AN ALTERNATIVE: 364   FOR ENTERTAINING: 352

Pad Thai Noodles with Mushrooms

SERVES 4

125 g/4 oz flat rice noodles
  or rice vermicelli
1 tbsp vegetable oil
2 garlic cloves, peeled
  and finely chopped
1 medium egg,
  lightly beaten
225 g/8 oz mixed

mushrooms, including
  shiitake, oyster, field,
  brown and wild
  mushrooms
2 tbsp lemon juice
1½ tbsp Thai fish sauce
½ tsp sugar
½ tsp cayenne pepper

2 spring onions, trimmed
  and cut into 2.5 cm/1 inch
  pieces
50 g/2 oz fresh beansprouts

To garnish:
chopped roasted peanuts
freshly chopped coriander

Cook the noodles according to the packet instructions. Drain well and reserve.

Heat a wok or large frying pan. Add the oil and garlic. Fry until just golden. Add the egg and stir quickly to break it up.

Cook for a few seconds before adding the noodles and mushrooms. Scrape down the sides of the pan to ensure they mix with the egg and garlic.

Add the lemon juice, fish sauce, sugar, cayenne pepper, spring onions and half of the beansprouts, stirring quickly all the time. Cook over a high heat for a further 2–3 minutes until everything is heated through.

Turn on to a serving plate. Top with the remaining beansprouts. Garnish with the chopped peanuts and coriander and serve immediately.

Try this: FOR AN ALTERNATIVE: 128   FOR ENTERTAINING: 350

Vegetable Biryani

SERVES 6

2 tbsp vegetable oil, plus a
  little extra for brushing
2 large onions, peeled and
  thinly sliced lengthwise
2 garlic cloves, peeled and
  finely chopped
2.5 cm/1 inch piece fresh
  root ginger, peeled and
  finely grated
1 small carrot, peeled and
  cut into sticks

1 small parsnip, peeled
  and diced
1 small sweet potato chunks,
  peeled and diced
1 tbsp medium curry paste
225 g/8 oz basmati rice
4 ripe tomatoes, peeled,
  deseeded and diced
600 ml/1 pint vegetable
  stock
175 g/6 oz cauliflower florets

50 g/2 oz peas, thawed
  if frozen
salt and freshly ground
  black pepper

To garnish:
roasted cashew nuts
raisins
fresh coriander leaves

Preheat the oven to 200°C/400°F/Gas Mark 6. Put 1 tablespoon of the vegetable oil in a large bowl with the onions and toss to coat. Lightly brush or spray a non-stick baking sheet with a little more oil. Spread half the onions on the baking sheet and cook at the top of the preheated oven for 25–30 minutes, stirring regularly, until golden and crisp. Remove from the oven and reserve for the garnish.

Meanwhile, heat a large flameproof casserole dish over a medium heat and add the remaining oil and onions. Cook for 5–7 minutes until softened and starting to brown. Add a little water if they start to stick. Add the garlic and ginger and cook for another minute, then add the carrot, parsnip and sweet potato. Cook the vegetables for a further 5 minutes. Add the curry paste and stir for a minute until everything is coated, then stir in the rice and tomatoes. After 2 minutes add the stock and stir well. Bring to the boil, cover and simmer over a very gentle heat for about 10 minutes. Add the cauliflower and peas and cook for 8–10 minutes, or until the rice is tender. Season to taste with salt and pepper. Serve garnished with the crispy onions, cashew nuts, raisins and coriander.

Try this: FOR AN ALTERNATIVE: 376   FOR ENTERTAINING: 332

Brown Rice Spiced Pilaf

SERVES 4

1 tbsp vegetable oil
1 tbsp blanched almonds,
  flaked or chopped
1 onion, peeled and
  chopped
1 carrot, peeled and diced
225 g/8 oz flat mushrooms,
  sliced thickly
¼ tsp cinnamon

large pinch dried chilli flakes
50 g/2 oz dried apricots,
  roughly chopped
25 g/1 oz currants
zest of 1 orange
350 g/12 oz brown
  basmati rice
900 ml/1½ pints
  vegetable stock

2 tbsp freshly
  chopped coriander
2 tbsp freshly snipped
  chives
salt and freshly ground
  black pepper
snipped chives, to garnish

Preheat the oven to 200°C/400°F/Gas Mark 6. Heat the oil in a large flameproof casserole dish and add the almonds. Cook for 1–2 minutes until just browning. Be careful as the nuts will burn very easily.

Add the onion and carrot. Cook for 5 minutes until softened and starting to turn brown. Add the mushrooms and cook for a further 5 minutes, stirring often.

Add the cinnamon and chilli flakes and cook for about 30 seconds before adding the apricots, currants, orange zest and rice.

Stir together well and add the stock. Bring to the boil, cover tightly and transfer to the preheated oven. Cook for 45 minutes until the rice and vegetables are tender.

Stir the coriander and chives into the pilaf and season to taste with salt and pepper. Garnish with the extra chives and serve immediately.a

Try this: FOR AN ALTERNATIVE: 374   FOR ENTERTAINING: 98

Creamy Vegetable Korma

SERVES 4-6

2 tbsp ghee or vegetable oil
1 large onion, peeled
  and chopped
2 garlic cloves, peeled
  and crushed
2.5 cm/1 inch piece of root
  ginger, peeled and grated
4 cardamom pods
2 tsp ground coriander
1 tsp ground cumin

1 tsp ground turmeric
finely grated rind and juice
  of ½ lemon
50 g/2 oz ground almonds
400 ml/14 fl oz
  vegetable stock
450 g/1 lb potatoes,
  peeled and diced
450 g/1 lb mixed vegetables,
  such as cauliflower,

carrots and turnip,
  cut into chunks
150 ml/¼ pint double cream
3 tbsp freshly chopped
  coriander
salt and freshly ground
  black pepper
naan bread, to serve

Heat the ghee or oil in a large saucepan. Add the onion and cook for 5 minutes. Stir in the garlic and ginger and cook for a further 5 minutes, or until soft and just beginning to colour.

Stir in the cardamom, ground coriander, cumin and turmeric. Continue cooking over a low heat for 1 minute, stirring. Stir in the lemon rind and juice and almonds. Blend in the vegetable stock. Slowly bring to the boil, stirring occasionally.

Add the potatoes and vegetables. Bring back to the boil, then reduce the heat, cover and simmer for 35–40 minutes, or until the vegetables are just tender. Check after 25 minutes and add a little more stock if needed.

Slowly stir in the cream and chopped coriander. Season to taste with salt and pepper. Cook very gently until heated through, but do not boil. Serve immediately with naan bread.

Try this: FOR AN ALTERNATIVE: 374 FOR ENTERTAINING: 368

Chinese Salad with Soy & Ginger Dressing

SERVES 4

1 head of Chinese cabbage	125 g/4 oz beansprouts	2.5 cm/1 inch piece root
200 g can water	2 tbsp freshly	ginger, peeled and
chestnuts, drained	chopped coriander	finely grated
6 spring onions, trimmed	For the soy &	zest and juice of 1 lemon
4 ripe but firm	ginger dressing:	salt and freshly ground
cherry tomatoes	2 tbsp sunflower oil	black pepper
125 g/4 oz mangetout	4 tbsp light soy sauce	crusty white bread, to serve

Rinse and finely shred the Chinese cabbage and place in a serving dish.

Slice the water chestnuts into small slivers and cut the spring onions diagonally into 2.5 cm/ 1 inch lengths, then split lengthwise into thin strips. Cut the tomatoes in half and then slice each half into three wedges and reserve.

Simmer the mangetout in boiling water for 2 minutes until beginning to soften, drain and cut in half diagonally. Arrange the water chestnuts, spring onions, mangetout, tomatoes and beansprouts on top of the shredded Chinese cabbage. Garnish with the freshly chopped coriander.

Make the dressing by whisking all the ingredients together in a small bowl until mixed thoroughly. Serve with the bread and the salad.

Try this: FOR AN ALTERNATIVE: 340   FOR ENTERTAINING: 328

Index

Index